the Bistro Cookbook

The Bistro Cookbook

Everyday cuisine from the French country kitchen

First published in 2012

LOVE FOOD is an imprint of Parragon Books Ltd

Parragon
Queen Street House
4 Queen Street
Bath BA1 1HE, UK

ISBN: 978-1-4454-7512-7
Printed in China

Design by Tracy Killick
New photography by Clive Streeter
New food styling by Teresa Goldfinch
New recipes by Beverly Le Blanc
Commissioning Editor: Cheryl Thomas

Notes for the reader

This book uses standard kitchen measuring spoons and cups. All spoon and cup measurements are level unless otherwise indicated. Unless otherwise stated, milk is assumed to be whole, eggs are large, individual vegetables are medium, and pepper is freshly ground black pepper. Unless otherwise stated, all root vegetables should be washed and peeled before using.

Garnishes and serving suggestions are all optional and not necessarily included in the recipe ingredients or method. The times given are only an approximate guide. Preparation times differ according to the techniques used by different people and the cooking times may also vary from those given. Optional ingredients, variations, or serving suggestions have not been included in the calculations.

Recipes using raw or very lightly cooked eggs should be avoided by infants, the elderly, pregnant women, and people with weakened immune systems. Pregnant and breast-feeding women are advised to avoid eating peanuts and peanut products. People with nut allergies should be aware that some of the prepared ingredients used in the recipes in this book may contain nuts. Always check the packaging before use.

Picture acknowledgments

The publisher would like to thank the following for permission to reproduce copyright material on the cover and following pages:
Cover: Getty/Studer-T., Veronika (front image); Fotolia/Infinity (wooden background); Fotolia/Infinity (PLC spoon image).
Endpapers: Fotolia/Marek.

Linen backgrounds, textured borders and decorative frames (throughout): Fotolia/Tombaky; CG Textures; Fotolia/Robynmac.

Page 1: Fotolia Igor Kolos;
Page 6: Richard Bertinet;
Page 13: Fotolia Robynmac;
Page 51: iStockphotos Two Humans;
Page 91: iStockphotos Two Humans;
Page 129: Fotolia Elena Moiseeva;
Page 153: iStockphotos Two Humans;
Page 181: Fotolia Zwei Kochloffel.

Contents

Foreword by Richard Bertinet

My love affair with bistro cooking goes back to my childhood in Brittany. It was very much a family affair. My uncle, Tonton Dominic, owned the Café de la Place, our local café bistro, and various other family members worked with him, so we ate there often. I have vivid memories of it even now. I loved the strong smell of pastis, and the way the light in the dining room filtered through a smoky haze; this was France in the 1970s after all.

The menu featured the plentiful local seafood: Crevettes Grises or Bigornneaux sprinkled with sea salt flakes to pick at as an appetizer, Broiled Lamb served simply with some Dauphinoise Potatoes and Green Beans, and, for me, always Crème Caramel for dessert. The room was busy, ordinary people from all walks of life chatting and sharing the news of the day over lunch or dinner. The food was simple, with robust flavors and all based on local seasonal ingredients. Not because it was fashionable, but because they were easily available and economical. Dishes would be made slowly and steeped with flavor but they would be served quickly.

Many French bistros are little more than a husband-and-wife affair, particularly out in the countryside. One partner cooks (another reason why bistro dishes are simple and easy to manage!) while the other runs the "front of house" service. Dining rooms are rarely grand and, on occasion, are little more than an extension of the family dining room. Ten years ago, I was driving through France with my wife (who was obviously pregnant, with our eldest son). We arrived in a village a little too late for lunch, but clearly hot and tired. The owners of a tiny, one-room bistro took pity on us and, despite the late hour, agreed to cook for us. Nothing special—just the menu du jour: some Pork and Roasted Tomatoes. To this day, it is one of the most memorable meals we have shared. The pork was roasted in a pan, succulent, perfectly seasoned and with a few herbs. The tomatoes, similarly roasted, had a deep rich flavor. Ever so simple but still so utterly delicious.

I started my career as a baker in France, but when I came to England in the 1980s no one was making artisan bread, so I looked for work as a chef. My cooking was influenced by the food of my childhood. Even when called upon to produce more elaborate creations, they were, at their roots, simple bistro dishes.

When we opened the cooking school in 2005, we introduced two regular French cooking classes based on the bistro cooking tradition: Classic Bistro Cooking to cover the national staples, such as Moules Marinères and Coq au Vin, and a French Country Cooking class to explore the specialties of the different French regions: the hearty stews and terrines from the Southwest, the Mediterranean specialties from Provence, and seafood from Normandy and Brittany. These classes are still as popular today as they were when we first launched them. I think this is primarily because the bistro style of cooking is so accessible. It is the type of food that most of us want to cook and share at home. And, as so much of it can be prepared ahead, it is also perfect for entertaining. Most bistro dishes can be prepared earlier in the day or the day before at your leisure. They store well and, indeed, leaving them overnight allows the flavors to develop. They are ready when you're ready and dinner can be served "quickly" in true bistro tradition.

Even if you are new to French cooking, I urge you to pick up this book and try it. This is not haute cuisine or complicated food. It is honest, real food, and this book is packed full of dishes that everyone can attain. Better still, get the family in the kitchen with you and create your own family bistro at home.

Introduction

Defining the Bistro

Bistros are a cornerstone of French culinary tradition. The French—whether they are young or old, sophisticated urbanites or rural agricultural workers—have a special place in their hearts for the unpretentious, hearty, and always satisfying food served in bistros across the country.

The iconic bistro image is of a cozy neighborhood restaurant, with a zinc-topped bar, paper or checkered tablecloths, flickering candlelight, and the daily specials displayed on chalkboards. In reality, however, the term "bistro" (sometimes also spelled "bistrot") is applied to a variety of establishments—from small cafés to world-famous Paris institutions, such as Chez L'Ami Louis, which is nothing less than a proper restaurant.

Perhaps, surprisingly, when you consider the significance of bistros in French cultural life, there is little agreement on when exactly bistros first started. Food historians date the use of the term "bistro" only from the end of the nineteenth or beginning of the twentieth century and agree this relaxed style of dining and drinking began in Paris. Other than that, there is little consensus.

It is a popular but apocryphal story to say bistros are so named because of the similar sound of the word to the Russian word for "quick." According to the legend, Russian soldiers occupying Paris after the fall of Napoleon in 1815 were said to shout "quick, quick" when walking into cafés in search of something to eat and drink and, thus, the bistro was born. Unfortunately, this story is untrue—the word "bistro" is not recorded until several decades later.

In the hierarchy of French restaurants, bistros and brasseries are often regarded as interchangeable. They both offer unpretentious, solid cooking at reasonable prices but there is a defining difference—bistros tend to be small and cozy, while brasseries are big and bustling.

One consistent theme that applies to all bistros, however, is the traditional, home-style food they serve. Classics, such as Coq au Vin, Cassoulet, Boeuf Bourguignon, Poule au Pot, Soupe à l'Oignon, and Croque Monsieur, are among the familiar stars of bistro menus.

Another feature of all bistros is their relaxed ambiance. The great and the good of the political establishment can be sitting at the next table, as can a neighborhood tradesperson. Bistros provide an

egalitarian style of dining not offered by the more refined haute cuisine restaurants. In the smallest bistros, *le patron* or *la patronne* (the owner) can be the person taking your order or cooking your meal—or doing both jobs!

France on a Plate

One of the joys of bistro dining, wherever you are in France, is that menus usually feature a *plat du jour*, or dish of the day. Always consider this option when deciding what to order because it will offer excellent value for your money. It will showcase the best of seasonal ingredients and will be inspired by the chef's visit to the local market. Look also to see if a particular dish is specified as a *spécialité de la maison*, or house special.

While traveling around France, bistro dining offers a wonderful way to sample classic French food and regional specialties. Soupe au Pistou and Tapenade are as much a fixture of Provençal menus, for example, as Quiche Lorraine is in Alsace and

Bouillinade is in the Pyrenees. You will undoubtedly also find a good selection of inexpensive local wines, available by the glass or carafe, as well as the more expensive bottled wines. When you study the menu in a French bistro and can't decide what to order, take a look around. You'll soon see what the locals are eating and that is certain to be an excellent choice.

In Paris, bistro meal service can run throughout the day, but in the countryside more rigid menu times will be observed. *Le déjeuner*, or lunch, is often served from noon until 2:30 p.m., and *le dîner*, or the evening meal, is served from 7 p.m. until 10:30 or 11 p.m. Do not just assume all bistros are open seven days a week, because some close on Sunday (and maybe Saturday, too) if there isn't a local food market. Many bistro owners also observe the French tradition of closing for part or all of August.

It is the simplicity of bistro food that makes it ideal for recreating at home. In France, this style of food is known as *cuisine bourgeoise*. As you look through this beautifully photographed collection of tempting recipes, you will only find familiar ingredients and basic cooking techniques. This is not the food of Michelin-starred kitchens— it is food to enjoy with family and friends.

Bon appétit!

chapter one
Appetizers

Vichyssoise
Leek & Potato Soup

❖ Serves 6
❖ Prepared in 15–20 minutes, plus chilling
❖ Cooks in 30–40 minutes

3 large leeks
3 tablespoons salted butter or margarine
1 onion, thinly sliced
4 red-skinned potatoes, peeled and chopped

$3\frac{1}{2}$ cups vegetable stock
2 teaspoons lemon juice
pinch of ground nutmeg
$\frac{1}{4}$ teaspoon ground coriander
1 bay leaf
1 egg yolk
$\frac{2}{3}$ cup light cream
salt and white pepper
freshly snipped chives, to garnish

one Trim the leeks and remove most of the green part. Slice the white part of the leeks finely.

Two Melt the butter in a large saucepan over medium heat. Add the leeks and onion and sauté, stirring occasionally, for about 5 minutes, without browning.

three Add the potatoes, stock, lemon juice, nutmeg, coriander, and bay leaf to the pan, season with salt and pepper, and bring to a boil. Cover and simmer for about 30 minutes, or until all the vegetables are soft.

four Cool the soup a little, remove and discard the bay leaf, and then process the soup in a food processor or blender until smooth. Pour into a clean pan.

five Blend the egg yolk into the cream, add a little of the soup to the mixture, and then whisk it all back into the soup and reheat gently, without boiling. Adjust the seasoning. Cool and then chill thoroughly in the refrigerator.

six Serve the soup garnished with freshly snipped chives.

Potage St Germain

Pea Soup

* ❖ Serves 4
* ❖ Prepared in
  15–20 minutes
* ❖ Cooks in 20–30 minutes

3 tablespoons salted butter
¼ cup finely chopped shallots
4 cups vegetable stock or water
2¾ cups shelled peas
pinch of sugar
¼ cup crème fraîche
salt and pepper
croutons and blue cheese,
   such as Roquefort, crumbled,
   to serve

one

Two

Two

one Melt the butter in a large saucepan over medium heat. Add the shallots and sauté, stirring, for 2–3 minutes, or until soft. Add the stock, peas, and sugar, season with salt and pepper, and bring to a boil, uncovered. Simmer for 15–20 minutes, or until the peas are tender.

Two Strain the peas and reserve the cooking liquid. Process the peas in a food processor or blender, then return the puree to the pan. Gradually stir in the cooking liquid until you have the desired consistency.

Three Reheat the soup. Stir in the crème fraîche and adjust the seasoning. Serve immediately with blue cheese and croutons sprinkled over the soup.

17

Soupe à l'oignon
French Onion Soup

✤ Serves 6
✤ Prepared in 10–12 minutes
✤ Cooks in 1½ hours

3 tablespoons olive oil
6 onions (about 1½ pounds), thinly sliced
4 garlic cloves, 3 chopped and 1 halved

1 teaspoon sugar
2 teaspoons chopped fresh thyme, plus extra sprigs to garnish
2 tablespoons all-purpose flour
½ cup dry white wine
9 cups vegetable stock
6 slices baguette
3 cups shredded Gruyère cheese

one Heat the oil in a large, heavy saucepan over medium–low heat, add the onions and cook, stirring occasionally, for 10 minutes, or until they are just beginning to brown. Stir in the chopped garlic, sugar, and chopped thyme, then reduce the heat and cook, stirring occasionally, for 30 minutes, or until the onions are golden brown.

Two Sprinkle in the flour and cook, stirring continuously, for 1–2 minutes. Stir in the wine. Gradually stir in the stock and bring to a boil, skimming off any scum that rises to the surface, then reduce the heat and simmer for 45 minutes.

Three Meanwhile, preheat the broiler to medium. Toast the bread on both sides under the broiler, then rub the toast with the cut edges of the halved garlic clove.

four Ladle the soup into six ovenproof bowls set on a baking sheet. Float a piece of toast in each bowl and divide the shredded cheese among them. Place under the preheated broiler for 2–3 minutes, or until the cheese has just melted. Garnish with thyme sprigs and serve immediately.

Soupe au pistou
Vegetable Soup with Pistou Sauce

✤ Serves 4–6
✤ Prepared in 20 minutes
✤ Cooks in 1¼ hours

4 tomatoes, peeled, seeded,
   and diced
1 cup bite-size green beans
   pieces
1 fennel bulb, quartered
   and sliced
1 carrot, diced
1 zucchini, diced
1 bouquet garni of fresh
   flat-leaf parsley, thyme
   sprigs, and a bay leaf,
   tied with string
pinch of sugar
2 tablespoons tomato paste
½ cup shelled fava beans or
   shelled peas
1 (15-ounce) can navy beans,
   drained and rinsed
2 tablespoons small dried soup
   pasta, such as ditalini, or
   broken spaghetti pieces
salt and pepper

Pistou sauce
3 garlic cloves,
   coarsely chopped
2 cups basil leaves
⅓ cup freshly grated Parmesan
   cheese, plus extra to serve
pinch of coarse sea salt
6 tablespoons extra virgin olive
   oil, plus extra to serve

one

Two

three

one Put the tomatoes, green beans, fennel, carrot, zucchini, bouquet garni, sugar, and tomato paste into a large, heavy saucepan. Pour in enough water to cover the vegetables by 3 inches and season generously with salt and pepper. Cover the pan and bring to a boil, then stir well, reduce the heat to low, and simmer for 40–45 minutes, or until the vegetables are tender.

Two Meanwhile, to make the pistou sauce, crush the garlic in a large mortar. Add the basil, cheese, and salt and use the pestle to grind together until blended. Stir in the oil, tablespoon by tablespoon, then transfer to a bowl and set aside.

three Uncover the soup and increase the heat to a slow boil. Add the fava beans and canned beans and boil for 5–10 minutes, or until the fava beans are tender. Add the pasta and boil for 3–5 minutes, or according to the package directions, until the pasta is tender but still firm to the bite. The soup should be chunky, but stir in extra water with the beans if too much liquid has evaporated.

four Remove the bouquet garni. Stir in the pistou sauce. Taste and adjust the seasoning with salt and pepper, if necessary. Serve immediately with extra cheese and oil for adding at the table.

Soupe de poissons
Fish Soup

* ❖ Serves 6–8
* ❖ Prepared in 20–30 minutes, plus chilling and standing
* ❖ Cooks in 1½ hours

3½ cups olive oil

3 onions, coarsely chopped

3 carrots, coarsely chopped

3 celery stalks, coarsely chopped

1 fennel bulb, finely chopped

6 garlic cloves, coarsely chopped

1 bay leaf

⅔ cup vermouth

2 thyme sprigs

2¼ pounds whole fish, such as sea bass or pollock, gutted, filleted, but bones reserved

2¼ pounds bones from white fish

8 ounces unpeeled shrimp

10 cups water

juice and zest of 1 orange

pinch of saffron

toasted slices of baguette and grated Parmesan cheese, to serve

salt and pepper

Rouille

½ cup fresh bread crumbs soaked in 1 tablespoon water

3 garlic cloves, coarsely chopped

1 egg yolk

1 red chile, seeded and chopped

½ teaspoon salt

1 cup olive oil

one Place a large saucepan over medium heat and add the olive oil. Add the onions, carrots, celery, fennel, garlic, and bay leaf and cook gently for 20 minutes, or until soft. Add the vermouth and thyme and simmer for 2 minutes. Add the fish, fish bones, and shrimp and increase the heat. Cook, stirring, for 5 minutes, then add the water, orange juice and zest, and saffron. Bring to a boil and simmer for 45 minutes. Remove the bay leaf.

Two Meanwhile, make the rouille. Put all of the ingredients except for the olive oil into a food processor and process to a paste. Keep blending and add the olive oil in a slow stream until the consistency is that of a thick mayonnaise. Put in the refrigerator to chill.

three Crush the fish bones by processing the soup, in batches, in a food processor or blender. Let stand for 20 minutes. First strain through a colander, then through a fine strainer, then pour into a saucepan. Season with salt and pepper and reheat again to serve.

four Serve immediately with slices of toasted baguette and some grated Parmesan cheese to float on the soup and bowls of rouille alongside.

Soupe bretonne

Breton Fish Soup

- ✤ Serves 4
- ✤ Prepared in
  15–20 minutes
- ✤ Cooks in 40–50 minutes

2 teaspoons salted butter
1 large leek, thinly sliced
2 shallots, finely chopped
½ cup hard dry cider
1¼ cups fish stock
2 red-skinned or white round
  potatoes, peeled and diced
1 bay leaf
¼ cup all-purpose flour
1 cup whole milk
1 cup heavy cream
2 cups fresh sorrel leaves
12 ounces skinless monkfish
  or cod fillet, cut into 1-inch
  pieces
salt and pepper
baguette, to serve

one

two

four

one Melt the butter in a large saucepan over medium–low heat. Add the leek and shallots and cook for about 5 minutes, stirring frequently, or until they start to soften. Add the cider and bring to a boil.

two Stir in the stock, potatoes, and bay leaf with a large pinch of salt (unless the stock is salty) and bring back to a boil. Reduce the heat, cover, and cook gently for 10 minutes. Put the flour in a small bowl and slowly whisk in a few tablespoons of the milk to make a thick paste. Stir in a little more milk to make a smooth liquid.

three Adjust the heat so the soup bubbles gently. Stir in the flour mixture and cook, stirring frequently, for 5 minutes. Add the remaining milk and half of the cream. Continue cooking for about 10 minutes, or until the potatoes are tender.

four Chop the sorrel finely and combine with the remaining cream. (If using a food processor, chop and add the sorrel, then add the cream and process briefly.)

five Stir the sorrel cream into the soup and add the fish. Continue cooking, stirring occasionally, for about 3 minutes, or until the monkfish stiffens or the cod just begins to flake. Taste the soup and adjust the seasoning, if needed. Remove and discard the bay leaf, and serve the soup immediately with baguette.

Rillettes de porc
Pork Rillettes

❖ **Makes about 3¼ pounds**
❖ **Prepared in 15–20 minutes**
❖ **Cooks in 4–6 hours**

1 pound pork shoulder
2¼ pounds pork belly, rindless and boneless
1½ cups pork fat or lard
2 cups water
1 bouquet garni of 2 thyme sprigs, 2 parsley
   sprigs, and 3 bay leaves, tied with string
1 clove
½ teaspoon allspice
grating of fresh nutmeg
salt and pepper

To serve
pickles
mustard
baguette, sliced
  in half, rubbed
  with garlic halves, and toasted

one Cut the meat into 2-inch cubes and chop the fat into ½-inch cubes. Place the meat and fat in a large, heavy saucepan with the water, bouquet garni, and clove. (Don't be tempted to add any more water—this method is a type of gentle steaming. The pork should collapse, not boil).

Two Cover the pan and place it over the lowest heat your stove can create, using a heat diffuser if you've got one, or place it into low oven at 250°F. The pan should just be gently shuddering. Cook for 4–6 hours, checking and stirring about every 30 minutes to make sure that it's not burning. Remove from the heat and set aside to cool. Remove the bouquet garni and clove. While it's still slightly warm, add the spices and season with salt and pepper, then take two forks and gently tear apart the pork, mixing the fat with the meat. Be careful to keep the "planks" texture and avoid turning the meat into a paste.

three Cover the meat with a piece of wax paper or plastic wrap and refrigerate for 2–3 days before serving (although you could eat it right away). It will last for at least an additional week in the refrigerator. To serve, drop a spoonful onto a plate beside some pickles, mustard, and a baguette half.

Mini quiches lorraines
Quiche Lorraine Mini Tarts

✤ Makes 6
✤ Prepared in
   20–30 minutes
✤ Cooks in 40–50 minutes

9 ounces of store-bought
   rolled dough pie crust
all-purpose flour, for dusting
⅔ cup unsmoked lard leaves
   or diced ham
2 extra-large eggs
1 cup heavy cream
1 cup shredded Gruyère cheese
   or Swiss cheese
grating of fresh nutmeg
salt and pepper

one Remove the dough from the refrigerator about 10 minutes before you roll it out and preheat the oven to 400°F with a baking sheet inside.

Two Divide the dough into six equal pieces and roll out each on a lightly floured surface into 6–7-inch circles. Use to line six 4½-inch tart pans, leaving the excess dough hanging over the edges. Line the dough with parchment paper and fill with pie weights or dried beans. Put the tart pans on the hot baking sheet and bake in the oven for 5 minutes, or until the rim is set. Remove the paper and weights, then return the tart shells to the oven and bake for an additional 5 minutes, or until the bottoms look dry. Remove the tart shells from the oven and let cool on the baking sheet. Reduce the oven temperature to 375°F.

three Meanwhile, put the lard leaves in a skillet over low heat and sauté for 3 minutes, or until the fat begins to melt. Increase the heat to medium and continue sautéing until they are crisp. (Omit this step if you are using diced ham.)

four Sprinkle the lard leaves or ham over the pastry shell. Beat together the eggs, cream, and cheese, then season with the salt, pepper, and nutmeg. Carefully divide the filling among the pastry shells, then return the tarts to the oven to bake for 20–25 minutes, or until the filling is set and the pastry is golden brown. Transfer the quiches to a wire rack to cool completely, then remove from the pans before serving.

Two

three

four

Pâté de foie de volaille
Chicken Liver Pâté

❖ **Serves 4**
❖ **Prepared in 15–20 minutes**
❖ **Cooks in 12 minutes**

1½ sticks salted butter, plus 1½ sticks salted
  butter for clarifying (optional)
1 onion, finely chopped
1 garlic clove, minced
8 ounces chicken livers
½ teaspoon Dijon mustard
2 tablespoons brandy (optional)
salt and pepper
toasted whole-wheat bread, cut into strips,
  to serve

one Melt 6 tablespoons of the butter in a large skillet over medium heat and cook the onion for 3–4 minutes, or until soft and transparent. Add the garlic and continue to cook for an additional 2 minutes.

two Check the chicken livers and remove any discolored parts using a pair of scissors. Add the livers to the skillet and cook over high heat for 5–6 minutes, or until brown.

three Season well with salt and pepper and add the mustard and brandy, if using. Remove the skillet from the heat.

four Transfer the liver mixture to a blender or food processor and process until smooth. Dice the remaining 6 tablespoons of butter, add to the blender, and process again until creamy.

five Press the pâté into a serving dish or four small ramekins (individual ceramic dishes), smooth the surface, and cover. If it is to be kept for more than two days, you could cover the surface with the clarified butter. To make it, heat the butter in a saucepan until it melts. Let the sediment settle, then pour it over the pâté. Serve accompanied by strips of toast.

Tapenade

Olive Spread

✤ Serves 8
✤ Prepared in
   15–20 minutes
✤ No cooking

4 cups ripe black olives, pitted
2 tablespoons capers
2 teaspoons Dijon mustard
juice of ½ lemon
1 garlic clove, finely chopped
12 canned anchovy fillets,
   drained and soaked to
   remove the salt
handful of chopped fresh
   flat-leaf parsley, plus sprigs
   to garnish
2 tablespoons chopped fresh
   thyme (optional)
⅔ cup extra virgin olive oil,
   plus extra for brushing
salt and pepper
slices of baguette or ciabatta,
   to serve

one

one

two

one Put all the ingredients except for the salt and pepper into a
food processor and process until a good paste forms. Don't make it
too smooth—it should retain a little coarseness.

two Season with salt and pepper, keeping in mind that it may
already be salty from the capers, olives, and anchovies. Brush slices
of baguette with olive oil and toast them.

three Serve the tapenade with the slices of baguette and garnish
with sprigs of parsley.

Terrine de Truite
Trout Terrine

* Serves 4
* Prepared in 15–20 minutes
* Chills in 2–3 hours

8 ounces trout fillets
6 ounces smoked trout, finely sliced
⅔ cup cream cheese

1 tablespoon crème fraîche
1 tablespoon horseradish sauce
grated rind of 1 lemon
2 tablespoons chopped fresh flat-leaf parsley
1 tablespoon snipped fresh chives
salt and pepper
salad greens and whole-wheat toast, to serve

one Poach the trout fillets in a little water in a skillet for 3–4 minutes, or until cooked. Drain well and let cool.

two Line a small loaf pan with plastic wrap and then line with the smoked trout, leaving enough to overlap the top.

three Skin and flake the trout fillets and mix together with the cream cheese, crème fraîche, horseradish sauce, and lemon rind, and season with salt and pepper.

four Spoon a layer of the trout mixture into the lined pan. Sprinkle with the herbs, then cover with the remaining trout mixture. Fold over the smoked trout edges and cover with plastic wrap. Press down and chill in the refrigerator for 2–3 hours.

five Invert from the pan and slice carefully, using a sharp knife.

six Serve immediately, garnished with salad greens and accompanied by whole-wheat toast.

Brandade de morue

Salt Cod Puree

❖ **Serves 4**
❖ **Prepared in 35 minutes,
plus soaking**
❖ **Cooks in 10 minutes**

1 pound dried salt cod, ideally
  a center cut, soaked for
  24 hours with several changes
  of water
2 large garlic cloves
½ cup extra virgin olive oil
½ cup heavy cream
juice of 1 lemon
pepper
bottled roasted red peppers,
  drained and thinly sliced, and
  stuffed green olives to serve
  (optional)

Garlic toasts
24 baguette slices, each about
  ¼ inch thick
olive oil, for brushing
6 garlic cloves, halved

one

two

three

one Drain the cod and rinse well in cold water. Put the cod in a saucepan with water to cover, cover the pan, and slowly bring to a boil over high heat. Immediately remove the pan from the heat and let the salt cod stand, still covered, for 20 minutes.

two Meanwhile, to make the garlic toasts, preheat the broiler to high. Toast the bread on both sides until golden and crisp. Brush one side of each slice with oil and rub with garlic, pressing down firmly. Let cool completely.

three Drain the cod and remove the skin and all small bones. Flake the flesh into a food processor. Add the garlic and half of the oil and process until the mixture is blended. Slowly add the remaining oil and cream in alternate spoonfuls through the feed tube until the mixture is creamy and smooth. Season with the lemon juice and pepper.

four Reheat the puree, if desired, in a heatproof bowl set over a saucepan of simmering water, stirring continuously. Spread the puree on the toasts and serve with the sliced roasted peppers and olives on the side, if using.

Céleri rémoulade
Celeriac Salad with Crab

❖ **Serves 4**
❖ **Prepared in 20–25 minutes,**
   plus chilling
❖ **Cooks in 2 minutes**

1 head of celeriac, shredded
juice of 1 lemon
8 ounces fresh white crabmeat
chopped fresh dill or parsley, to garnish

mixed salad greens, to serve

Rémoulade dressing
²/₃ cup mayonnaise
1 tablespoon Dijon mustard
1½ teaspoons white wine vinegar
2 tablespoons capers in brine,
   well rinsed
salt and white pepper

one To make the dressing, put the mayonnaise in a bowl. Add the mustard, vinegar, and capers, season with salt and white pepper, and beat together—the mixture should be piquant with a strong mustard flavor. Cover and chill until required.

Two Bring a large saucepan of salted water to a rolling boil. Add the shredded celeriac and lemon juice to the water and blanch for 1½–2 minutes, or until it is just slightly tender. Rinse the celeriac well, then put it under cold running water to stop the cooking process. Use your hands to squeeze out the excess moisture, then pat the celeriac dry with paper towels or a clean dish towel.

three Stir the celeriac into the dressing, along with the crabmeat. Taste and adjust the seasoning, if necessary. Cover and chill for at least 30 minutes.

four When ready to serve, spoon into bowls with the mixed salad greens and garnish with dill or parsley.

39

Camembert au four

Baked Camembert

✤ Serves 4
✤ Prepared in
    4–5 minutes
✤ Cooks in 10–12 minutes

1 Camembert, about 8 ounces,
    ideally in a wooden box
2 tablespoons dry white
    vermouth
2 fresh thyme sprigs or
    2 bay leaves
4 slices pain au levain (French
    sourdough bread) or other
    sourdough bread, cut into
    strips and toasted, to serve
onion marmalade (optional),
    to serve

two

three

four

one Preheat the oven to 425°F and place a sheet of aluminum foil, shiny side up, on a baking sheet. Remove all the paper wrapping from the cheese and, if it came in a wooden box, return the wrapping to the bottom half of the box.

two Place the cheese in the center of the foil. Use a knife to cut a deep X in the center of the cheese. Spoon the vermouth over the cheese and let it steep in. Place the thyme sprigs on top.

three Wrap the foil around the cheese, sealing the edges to keep all the heat and moisture in. Bake in the preheated oven for 10–12 minutes, or until the cheese is soft when you unwrap it and press the top.

four Carefully unwrap the cheese, transfer back to the wooden box, and place on a serving plate. Put the plate in the center of the table and use a small spoon to scoop the soft cheese onto the strips of toast. Add a spoonful of onion marmalade to each serving, if using, and serve immediately while the cheese is still hot.

Soufflé
Cheese Soufflé

* ❖ Serves 4
* ❖ Prepared in 15 minutes
* ❖ Cooks in 30–35 minutes

1 tablespoon salted butter, melted
1 tablespoon finely grated Parmesan cheese
2 tablespoons salted butter
3 tablespoons all-purpose flour
1¼ cups whole milk
1 cup shredded cheddar cheese
1 teaspoon whole-grain mustard
grating of fresh nutmeg
4 extra-large eggs, separated
salt and pepper

one Preheat the oven to 400°F. Grease the bottom and sides of a soufflé dish with melted butter. Sprinkle the dish with the Parmesan, turning the dish in your hands so that all the surface is covered with the cheese.

Two Melt the remaining 2 tablespoons of butter in a saucepan (preferably nonstick) over medium heat. Add the flour, mix well using a wooden spoon, and cook for 1 minute, stirring continuously. Remove from the heat and stir in the milk gradually until you have a smooth consistency.

three Return the pan to low heat and continue to stir while the sauce comes to a boil and thickens. Simmer gently, stirring continuously, for about 3 minutes, or until the sauce is creamy and smooth. Remove from the heat and stir in the cheddar cheese, mustard, and nutmeg. Season well with salt and pepper. Set aside to cool a little. Whisk the egg whites until soft peaks have formed but they are not too dry. Beat the egg yolks into the sauce mixture and then carefully stir in a little of the beaten egg white to slacken the mixture. Carefully fold in the remaining egg whites, then turn into the prepared dish. Place on a baking sheet and cook in the preheated oven for 25–30 minutes, or until well risen and golden brown. Serve immediately.

Asperges à la sauce hollandaise
Asparagus with Hollandaise Sauce

✤ Serves 4
✤ Prepared in
   10–15 minutes
✤ Cooks in 15–20 minutes

1½ pounds asparagus, trimmed

Hollandaise sauce
¼ cup white wine vinegar
½ tablespoon finely chopped
   shallots
5 black peppercorns
1 bay leaf
3 extra-large egg yolks
1¼ sticks unsalted butter,
   finely diced
2 teaspoons lemon juice
salt
pinch of cayenne pepper

one Divide the asparagus into four bundles and tie each with kitchen string, crisscrossing the string from just below the tips to the bottom. Stand the bundles upright in a deep saucepan. Add boiling water to come three-quarters of the way up the stems, then cover with a loose tent of aluminum foil, shiny side down, inside the pan. Heat the water until bubbles appear around the side of the pan, then simmer for 10 minutes, or until the stems are just tender when pierced with the tip of a knife. Drain well.

Two Meanwhile, to make the hollandaise sauce, boil the vinegar, shallots, peppercorns, and bay leaf in a saucepan over high heat until reduced to 1 tablespoon. Cool slightly, then strain into a heatproof bowl that will fit over a saucepan of simmering water.

three Beat the egg yolks into the bowl. Set the bowl over the pan of simmering water and whisk the egg yolks continuously until they are thick enough to leave a trail on the surface.

four Do not let the water boil. Gradually beat in the butter, piece by piece, whisking continuously until the sauce is like soft mayonnaise. Stir in the lemon juice, then season with salt and cayenne pepper. Serve the sauce immediately with the asparagus.

one

Two

three

45

Figues au bleu
Figs with Blue Cheese

✤ Serves 6
✤ Prepared in 10 minutes
✤ Cooks in 10–15 minutes

½ cup granulated sugar
¾ cup whole almonds,
    blanched or unblanched
butter, for greasing
12 ripe figs
12 ounces blue cheese, cubed
extra virgin olive oil, to serve

one To make the caramelized almonds, put the sugar in a saucepan over medium–high heat. Stir until the sugar melts and turns golden brown and bubbles; do not stir once the mixture starts to bubble.

Two Remove from the heat and add the almonds one at a time. Quickly turn with a fork until coated; if the caramel hardens, return the saucepan to the heat. Transfer each almond to a lightly greased baking sheet once it is coated. Let stand until cool and firm.

three To serve, slice the figs into quarters and arrange eight quarters on each plate. Coarsely chop the almonds by hand. Place cubes of the blue cheese on each plate and sprinkle with chopped almonds. Serve immediately, with the oil drizzled lightly over the top.

Poires pochées
Poached Pears in Red Wine

✤ Serves 4
✤ Prepared in
    12–15 minutes,
    plus chilling
✤ Cooks in 20–25 minutes

2 cups dry red wine, such
    as Merlot
3 tablespoons firmly packed
    light brown sugar
3 firm pears, such as Bosc,
    peeled, quartered, and cored
4 cups mixed salad greens
¼ cup coarsely chopped
    walnut halves
2 ounces Parmesan cheese
    shavings
baguette, to serve (optional)

Vinaigrette
2 tablespoons extra virgin
    olive oil
1 tablespoon walnut oil
1 tablespoon red wine vinegar
    or cider vinegar
½ teaspoon Dijon mustard
½ teaspoon sugar
salt and pepper

one

three

four

one Prepare the pears up to a day, but at least 4 hours, in advance. Mix together the wine and sugar in a saucepan over medium heat, stirring until the sugar dissolves. Reduce the heat to low, add the pears, and simmer for 5–10 minutes, or until they are tender but still holding their shape. Using a slotted spoon, transfer the pears to a bowl and let cool.

Two Bring the syrup to a boil and boil until reduced to about 1/2 cup. Remove the syrup from the heat and set aside to cool. Spoon the cooled syrup over the pears, cover with plastic wrap, and chill for up to a day, stirring occasionally, until the pears take on a deep garnet color.

three Meanwhile, to make the vinaigrette, put the olive oil, walnut oil, vinegar, mustard, and sugar in a bowl. Season with salt and pepper and whisk until well blended, then set aside.

four Put the salad greens and walnuts in a bowl. Whisk the vinaigrette again if it has separated, then add to the bowl and toss the greens until they are lightly coated. Add the cheese shavings and gently toss again.

five Divide the salad among four plates. Drain the pears from the syrup, arrange three quarters on top of each plate of salad, and serve immediately with a baguette alongside, if using.

Bœuf bourguignon
Beef Bourguignon

✤ Serves 6
✤ Prepared in
   15–20 minutes
✤ Cooks in 3½ hours

2 tablespoons olive oil
6 ounces unsmoked bacon,
   sliced into thin strips
3 pounds boneless beef chuck
   or beef round cut into 2-inch
   pieces
2 carrots, sliced
2 onions, chopped
2 garlic cloves, minced
3 tablespoons all-purpose flour
3 cups red wine
1½–2 cups beef stock
1 bouquet garni of 2 thyme
   sprigs, 2 parsley sprigs, and
   3 bay leaves, tied with string
1 teaspoon salt
¼ teaspoon pepper
3 tablespoons salted butter
12 ounces pearl onions
3½ cups white button
   mushrooms
chopped fresh flat-leaf parsley,
   to garnish
mashed potatoes, to serve

one

Two

Three

one Heat the oil in a large casserole dish over medium heat. Add the bacon and brown for 2–3 minutes. Remove with a slotted spoon and set aside. Add the beef to the dish, in batches, and cook until browned. Drain and set aside with the bacon. Add the carrots and chopped onions to the dish and cook for 5 minutes. Add the garlic and sauté until just golden. Return the meat and bacon to the casserole dish. Sprinkle the flour over the meat and cook for 1 minute, stirring. Add the wine, enough stock to cover, the bouquet garni, and salt and pepper. Bring to a boil, cover, and simmer gently for 3 hours.

Two Heat half of the butter in a skillet. Add the pearl onions, cover, and cook until softened. Remove with a slotted spoon and keep warm. Heat the remaining butter in the skillet. Add the mushrooms and sauté briefly. Set aside the mushrooms and keep warm.

three Remove the casserole dish from the heat and strain the casserole liquid through a strainer into a clean saucepan. Wipe the casserole dish with paper towels and transfer the meat mixture, mushrooms, and onions to the dish. Discard the bouquet garni. Remove the surface fat from the casserole liquid, simmer for 1–2 minutes to reduce the liquid, then pour it over the meat and vegetables in the dish. Serve immediately, garnished with parsley and with mashed potatoes on the side.

Steak Tartare

Steak Tartare

* Serves 4
* Prepared in 20–25 minutes, plus chilling
* No cooking

1 pound top-quality filet mignon or
   tenderloin steak
2 tablespoons finely chopped fresh
   flat-leaf parsley
2 tablespoons finely chopped capers
2 tablespoons finely chopped shallots
2 tablespoons finely chopped gherkin pickles
4 dashes Tabasco sauce
4 dashes Worcestershire sauce
2 tablespoons Dijon mustard
1 teaspoon fine salt
4 egg yolks (kept separate)
French fries or boiled potatoes, to serve

one Make sure all the ingredients, cutting board, and mixing bowl are chilled—put them in the refrigerator for 20 minutes before you start preparing and take them out when ready to use.

two Chop the steak by hand, until ground. Take your time, and don't mush the steak or it will lose its texture and seep all its juices. Lay the meat in the chilled bowl. Add all the remaining ingredients, except the egg yolks, and mix them into the beef with a fork.

three Shape the mixture into four round mounds and make an indentation in the middle of each. Place in the refrigerator until ready to serve.

four When you are ready to serve, place each mound in the middle of a plate and lay an egg yolk in the indentation.

five Serve with French fries and tell your guests to mix the egg yolk into the beef.

Steak frites
Steak & French Fries

✤ **Serves 4**
✤ **Prepared in**
   20–25 minutes
✤ **Cooks in 45 minutes–**
   1 hour

1 bunch of watercress, plus
   extra to garnish
6 tablespoons unsalted butter,
   softened
4 tenderloin steaks, about
   8 ounces each
4 teaspoons Tabasco sauce
salt and pepper

French fries
4 russet potatoes, peeled
2 tablespoons sunflower oil

one To make the French fries, preheat the oven to 400°F. Cut the potatoes into thick, even sticks. Rinse them under cold running water, then dry well on a clean dish towel. Place in a bowl, add the oil, and toss together until coated.

Two Spread the potatoes on a baking sheet and cook in the preheated oven for 40–45 minutes, turning once, or until golden.

Three Using a sharp knife, finely chop enough watercress to fill ¼ cup. Place the butter in a small bowl and beat in the chopped watercress with a fork until completely incorporated. Cover with plastic wrap and let chill in the refrigerator until required.

four Preheat a ridged grill pan to high. Sprinkle each steak with 1 teaspoon of the Tabasco sauce, rubbing it in well. Season with salt and pepper.

five Cook the steaks on the preheated grill pan for 2½ minutes on each side for rare, 4 minutes on each side for medium, and 6 minutes on each side for well done. Transfer to serving plates and serve immediately, topped with the watercress butter and accompanied by the French fries. Garnish with watercress.

one

three

five

Bœuf en Daube

Beef in Red Wine Stew

❖ Serves 6
❖ Prepared in 20–30 minutes,
   plus marinating
❖ Cooks in 3½ hours

2¼ pounds center cut beef shanks,
   cut into 16 large chunks
1 large carrot, diced
2 large onions, coarsely chopped
2 celery stalks, coarsely chopped
5 garlic cloves, coarsely chopped
bouquet garni of 2 thyme sprigs, 4 bay leaves,
   and 2 parsley sprigs, tied with string

3 cups red wine
2 tablespoons all-purpose flour
¼ cup lard or vegetable oil
4 parsnips, cut into chunks
5 cups chicken stock
7 cups large white button mushroom pieces
   (about 1 pound)
9 white round potatoes (2¼ pounds),
   peeled and chopped
1¼ sticks salted butter
½ cup heavy cream
salt and pepper
chopped fresh flat-leaf parsley, to garnish

one The day before, put the beef, carrot, onions, celery, garlic, bouquet garni, and wine into a bowl and marinate overnight. Remove the meat from the marinade and pat dry. Strain, reserving the wine, and set aside the vegetables and bouquet garni.

Two Mix the flour with some salt and pepper in a bowl and toss the beef in it. Put 2 tablespoons of the lard into a large casserole dish and place over high heat. When the fat is smoking, add two pieces of the beef and quickly brown on all sides, without letting it cook through. Remove and set aside, and continue with the rest of the beef.

Three Put the remaining lard into the casserole dish, add the parsnips, and brown them over high heat. Add the browned meat, reserved wine, reserved vegetables, stock, bouquet garni, and mushrooms and mix through. Place, uncovered, in a cold oven and heat to 275°F. Cook for 1 hour, then cover and cook for an additional 2 hours. Remove the lid from the casserole dish 45 minutes before the beef is cooked.

four Bring a large saucepan of lightly salted water to a boil, add the potatoes, and cook for 20 minutes, or until tender. Drain, then pass through a potato ricer with the butter. Add some salt and the cream and mix together. Place the mashed potatoes on warm plates, ladle the daube on top (removing the bouquet garni), and sprinkle with a little parsley.

Escalopes de veau

Veal Scallops with Marsala

✤ Serves 2
✤ Prepared in
  10–15 minutes
✤ Cooks in 3 minutes

4 veal cutlets, about
  2½ ounces each
1 tablespoon all-purpose flour
3 tablespoons olive oil
⅔ cup Marsala wine
salt and pepper
handful of chopped fresh
  flat-leaf parsley, to garnish
mashed potatoes or green
  salad, to serve

one

Two

three

one Put each veal cutlet between two pieces of plastic wrap or inside a plastic food bag and, using a rolling pin, gently beat out until ⅛ inch thick.

Two Season the scallops well with salt and pepper and dust with the flour.

three Heat the oil in a large skillet, add the scallops, and cook over high heat for 1 minute on each side, or until lightly browned. Add the wine and let the liquid bubble around the scallops for 1 minute.

four Serve immediately with the pan juices poured over the meat. Garnish with parsley and serve accompanied by mashed potatoes or a green salad.

Côtes de veau

Veal Chops

❖ **Serves 4**
❖ **Prepared in 5 minutes,**
   plus soaking
❖ **Cooks in 20–30 minutes**

4 veal chops on the bone, each weighing
   about 6 ounces
olive oil, for rubbing
salt and pepper
chopped fresh flat-leaf parsley, to garnish
Sautéed Potatoes (see page 174),
   to serve (optional)

Mushroom sauce
1 cup red vermouth
1 ounce dried porcini, soaked in boiling water
   for 10 minutes
4 tablespoons salted butter, plus an extra pat
1 shallot, finely chopped
6 ounces cremini mushrooms or button
   mushrooms, sliced
1½ cups beef stock
freshly grated nutmeg, to taste
salt and pepper

one To make the sauce, put the vermouth into a small saucepan. Bring to a boil and cook until it is reduced by half, then set aside. Meanwhile, strain the porcini through a coffee filter or strainer lined with cheesecloth and set the liquid aside. Rinse the porcini, then finely chop and set aside.

Two Melt the butter in a large skillet over medium heat. Add the shallot and sauté, stirring, for 2–3 minutes, or until soft. Add the porcini and cremini mushrooms, sprinkle with salt, and continue stirring until the moisture they release evaporates. Stir in the stock and reserved vermouth and porcini liquid and bring to a boil. Reduce the heat to low and simmer for 15–20 minutes, or until reduced. Season with nutmeg, salt, and pepper. Cover and keep hot until required.

Three While the sauce is simmering, preheat the broiler to high. Rub the chops on both sides with oil and place on the broiler rack, then sprinkle with salt and pepper. Cook about 4 inches from the heat for 4 minutes. Turn the chops over, sprinkle with salt and pepper, and broil for an additional 2–3 minutes for medium or 4 minutes for well done. Let the chops rest for 2 minutes. Add any accumulated juices and the pat of butter to the sauce and reheat, stirring. Transfer the chops to plates, spoon the mushroom sauce over them, and garnish with parsley. Serve immediately, with sautéed potatoes, if using.

Côtes de porc à la normande

Pork Chops with Apple Brandy & Apples

❖ Serves 4
❖ Prepared in 5–10 minutes
❖ Cooks in 40–45 minutes

6 tablespoons salted butter
2 firm apples, such as Granny Smith, peeled, cored, and each cut into 8 wedges
1 tablespoon granulated sugar
1 tablespoon sunflower oil
4 pork loin chops, about ¾ inch thick
2 shallots, chopped
½ tablespoon fresh thyme leaves or 1 teaspoon dried thyme
6 tablespoons Calvados, applejack, or other apple brandy
½ cup hard sweet or dry cider
1 cup heavy cream
salt and pepper
steamed baby broccoli, to serve

one

three

four

one Preheat the oven to its lowest temperature. Melt 2 tablespoons of the butter in a sauté pan or skillet large enough to hold the pork chops in a single layer, over medium heat. Add the apple wedges, sprinkle with the sugar, and sauté for 5–6 minutes, turning them several times, until golden brown. Transfer to an ovenproof dish and keep warm in the oven. Wipe out the pan.

Two Melt another 2 tablespoons of the butter with the oil in the pan over medium–high heat. Using a pair of tongs, cook the pork chops one at a time, fat edge down, until the fat is golden.

three Lay all the chops flat in the pan and cook for 5 minutes. Turn the chops over and cook for an additional 5–6 minutes, or until cooked through and tender. Transfer the chops to an ovenproof serving dish, cover with aluminum foil, and keep warm in the oven. Pour off the excess fat from the pan and wipe with paper towels.

four Melt the remaining butter in the pan. Add the shallots and thyme and sauté for 2–3 minutes, or until the shallots are soft, but not brown. Add the apple brandy and bring to a boil, scraping the sediment from the bottom of the pan. Stir in the cider and cream and return to a boil, stirring. Continue boiling until reduced by half, then season with salt and pepper.

five Spoon the sauce over the chops and garnish with the apple wedges. Serve immediately with the baby broccoli.

Croque monsieur
Toasted Ham &
Cheese Sandwich

✤ Serves 1
✤ Prepared in 5 minutes
✤ Cooks in 5–10 minutes

2 slices white bread, buttered
2 slices smoked ham
½ cup shredded Gruyère cheese or
   Swiss cheese
pat of salted butter, melted
salt and pepper
lightly dressed mixed green salad, to serve

one Preheat the broiler to high. Lay one piece of bread buttered side up and place the ham on top. Cover with two-thirds of the cheese and season with salt and pepper. Lay the other slice of bread on top, buttered side down. Brush the top side with the melted butter and place the bread, buttered side up, under the preheated broiler.

Two Broil until browned, then remove. Turn the sandwich over and scatter the remaining cheese on top. Return to the broiler and cook until the cheese is bubbling and browned. Remove and serve with a green salad.

Cassoulet

Pork & Lamb Casserole

✤ Serves 8
✤ Prepared in
   25–30 minutes,
   plus soaking
✤ Cooks in 3½ hours

2½ cups dried navy beans,
   soaked overnight
bouquet garni of 4 parsley
   sprigs, 2 thyme sprigs, and
   4 bay leaves, tied with string
1 celery stalk,
   coarsely chopped
3 onions, 1 quartered,
   2 thinly sliced
4 large garlic cloves,
   2 whole, 2 chopped
8 cups water
1 pound pork belly, skin
   removed and meat cut
   into 4 large chunks
1 pound shoulder of lamb,
   boned and cut into
   4 large chunks
2 tablespoons duck fat or
   vegetable oil
7 ounces thick cut bacon, cut
   into chunks
14 ounces Toulouse or pork
   sausage, sliced
2 tablespoons tomato paste
3 cups fresh bread crumbs
salt and pepper

two

two

three

one Drain and rinse the beans and put them in a large saucepan with the bouquet garni, celery, onion quarters, and whole garlic and season with salt and pepper. Add the water and bring to a boil. Skim off any foam, then reduce the heat to low. Gently simmer for 1 hour, uncovered.

two Meanwhile, preheat the oven to 350°F. Cut the pork and lamb into 1½-inch square pieces, then add the duck fat to a large, heavy saucepan and put over high heat. Add the pork belly and bacon and brown it all over. Remove and set aside, then repeat with the sausage, followed by the lamb. Set aside the sausage and lamb. Add the sliced onions, chopped garlic, and tomato paste and cook in the remaining fat for 2 minutes. Remove from the heat and let cool.

three Drain the beans, reserving the liquid but discarding the vegetables. In a large casserole dish, layer the beans and meat alternately until they're all used. Add the garlic-and-tomato paste mixture and enough of the bean-cooking liquid to almost cover the beans. Sprinkle the bread crumbs over the beans and cook in the oven, covered, for 1 hour. Reduce the heat to 275°F, remove the cover, and cook for an additional hour.

four Check the casserole is not too dry, adding a little heated bean liquid or water, if necessary. Serve immediately.

Navarin d'agneau
Spring Lamb Stew

❖ Serves 4– 6
❖ Prepared in 15–20 minutes
❖ Cooks in 1–1¼ hours

3 tablespoons salted butter
2 tablespoons sunflower oil, plus extra
   if needed
2 pounds boned shoulder of lamb,
   trimmed and cut into large chunks,
   any bones reserved
2 shallots, finely chopped
1 tablespoon sugar

4 cups lamb stock
2 tablespoons tomato paste
1 bouquet garni of several parsley and thyme
   sprigs, 1 bay leaf, and 1 small rosemary
   sprig, tied with string
8 new potatoes, scrubbed and halved, if large
4 young turnips, quartered
12 baby carrots, scrubbed
1 cup frozen peas
salt and pepper
chopped fresh flat-leaf parsley, to garnish
baguette, to serve

one Melt 2 tablespoons of the butter with the oil in a large skillet over medium heat. Add the lamb in batches to avoid overcrowding the skillet, and cook, stirring, until browned on all sides, adding extra oil, if necessary. Transfer the meat to a casserole dish.

Two Melt the remaining butter with the fat left in the skillet. Add the shallots and stir for 3 minutes, or until beginning to soften. Sprinkle with the sugar, increase the heat, and continue stirring until the shallots caramelize, being careful that they do not burn. Transfer to the casserole dish and remove any charred sediment from the bottom of the skillet. Add half of the stock to the skillet and bring to a boil, scraping the bottom of the skillet, then transfer this mixture into the casserole dish.

Three Add the remaining stock, tomato paste, bouquet garni, and bones, if any, to the casserole dish. Season with salt and pepper. Cover and bring to a boil. Reduce the heat and simmer for 45 minutes.

Four Add the potatoes, turnips, and carrots and continue simmering for 15 minutes. Add the peas, then uncover and simmer for an additional 5–10 minutes, or until the meat and all the vegetables are tender. Remove and discard the bones, if used, and the bouquet garni. Taste and adjust the seasoning, if necessary. Garnish with parsley and serve with a baguette for soaking up the juices.

Gigot D'agneau aux haricots verts
Roasted Leg of Lamb with Green Beans

* Serves 4–6
* Prepared in 10 minutes, plus marinating and resting
* Cooks in 1–1½ hours

3 garlic cloves, thinly sliced
1 leg of lamb, about 3 pounds, thinly slit all over
olive oil, for rubbing
½ cup dry red wine
½ cup water
2 tablespoons capers in brine, rinsed
3 cups trimmed green beans
2 tablespoons salted butter
salt and pepper

one Push the garlic into the slits in the lamb and rub the leg all over with salt and pepper. Place the lamb in a roasting pan, rub all over with oil, and set aside for at least 1 hour for the garlic to penetrate.

Two Meanwhile, preheat the oven to 450°F. Calculate the roasting time at 15 minutes per 1 pound 2 ounces plus 15 minutes for medium, and 20 minutes per 1 pound 2 ounces plus 20 minutes for well done.

three Roast the lamb in the preheated oven for 10 minutes, then reduce the oven temperature to 350°F and continue roasting for the calculated roasting time, until a meat thermometer reads about 130°F for medium–rare or 140°F for medium. Remove the lamb from the oven, transfer it to a carving dish, cover with a sheet of aluminum foil, and let rest for 20 minutes.

four While the lamb is resting, pour off any excess fat from the pan. Add the wine and water to the juices remaining in the pan and bring to a boil, scraping the sediment from bottom of the pan. Add the capers and heat through. Season this gravy with salt and pepper.

five About 10 minutes before serving, bring a saucepan of lightly salted water to a boil. Add the beans, bring back to a boil, and cook for 5–8 minutes, or until tender. Drain well and return to the pan. Add the butter and season with salt and pepper.

six Carve the lamb and serve immediately with the green beans, along with the gravy for spooning over the meat.

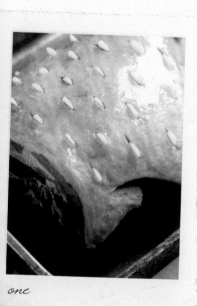
one

four

five

Lapin à la moutarde
Rabbit with Mustard Sauce

✤ Serves 4
✤ Prepared in 10 minutes, plus soaking
✤ Cooks in 1 hour

4 rabbit legs, about 10 ounces each, skinned
4 tablespoons salted butter
1 tablespoon sunflower oil, plus extra,
   if necessary
1 shallot, finely chopped

1 garlic clove, crushed
1 teaspoon dried thyme
½ cup dry white wine
1 cup chicken stock
3 tablespoons Dijon or whole-grain mustard
1 cup heavy cream
salt and pepper
chopped fresh flat-leaf parsley, to garnish
boiled green lentils, to serve (optional)

one At least 4 hours before cooking, soak the rabbit legs in enough salted water to cover them, then drain well and pat dry. Season with salt and pepper.

Two Melt 3 tablespoons of the butter with the oil in a large casserole dish over medium heat. Add the rabbit and cook each piece on both sides until brown, working in batches, if necessary, to avoid overcrowding the pan and adding extra oil, if necessary. Remove the rabbit pieces as they are browned and set aside.

Three Spoon off and discard all but ½ tablespoon of the fat. Add the shallot and sauté, stirring, for 2 minutes. Add the garlic and thyme and continue sautéing for an additional 2 minutes. Add the wine to the casserole dish and bring to a boil, using a spoon to scrape off any sediment stuck to the bottom of the dish, then boil until the liquid is reduced by half.

four Return the rabbit and any accumulated juices to the casserole dish and season with salt and pepper. Pour in the stock and add water, if necessary, so that all the ingredients are covered. Cover the casserole and bring to a boil. Reduce the heat to low and simmer for 40–45 minutes, or until the rabbit is tender.

five Transfer the rabbit to a warm, deep serving platter, using a slotted spoon, and keep warm. Stir the mustard and cream into the cooking juices. Bring to a boil and stir until the sauce thickens slightly and reduces. Stir in the remaining butter and adjust the seasoning, if necessary. Spoon the sauce over the rabbit pieces, garnish with parsley, and serve immediately with lentils, if using.

Poulet à la bretonne
Brittany Chicken Casserole

❖ Serves 6
❖ Prepared in
   15–20 minutes,
   plus soaking
❖ Cooks in 2½ hours

2½ cups dried beans, such as
   great Northern beans or
   navy beans, soaked overnight
   and drained
2 tablespoons salted butter
2 tablespoons olive oil
3 rindless bacon strips,
   chopped
2 pounds chicken legs
1 tablespoon all-purpose flour
1¼ cups hard cider
⅔ cup chicken stock
14 shallots
2 tablespoons honey, warmed
1½ cups chopped cooked beets
salt and pepper
baguette, to serve

two

three

five

one Preheat the oven to 325°F. Cook the beans in boiling water for 25 minutes, then drain thoroughly.

Two Heat the butter and oil in a large casserole dish. Add the bacon and chicken and cook for 5 minutes. Sprinkle with the flour, then add the cider and stock, stirring continuously to prevent lumps from forming. Season with salt and pepper and bring to a boil.

three Add the drained beans, then cover the casserole dish tightly and bake in the middle of the oven for 2 hours, or until the chicken is cooked through and the juices run clear when the tip of a sharp knife is inserted into the thickest part of the meat. About 15 minutes before the end of the cooking time, uncover the dish.

four Gently cook the shallots and honey in a skillet for 5 minutes, turning the shallots frequently, until golden.

five Add the shallots and beets to the casserole and return to the oven for the last 15 minutes of the cooking time. Serve immediately, with baguette.

Poule au pot
Chicken in a Pot

❖ **Serves 6**
❖ **Prepared in 15–20 minutes**
❖ **Cooks in 2½ hours**

6½ cups chicken stock
6½ cups water
bouquet garni of 4 parsley sprigs, 4 thyme
    sprigs, and 4 bay leaves, tied with string
1 teaspoon black peppercorns
6 ounces bacon, chopped into chunks
1 whole garlic bulb, halved
3 small leeks, cut into large chunks
3 carrots, cut into large chunks
3 celery stalks, cut into large chunks
3 turnips, cut into large chunks
6 pearl onions
4½–5½-pound chicken
1 small head of cabbage, cut into 6 pieces

12 small new potatoes, scrubbed
salt and pepper

Stuffing
1¼ cups dry bread crumbs
4 ounces chicken livers, finely chopped
1 shallot, finely chopped
1 egg
handful of chopped fresh flat-leaf parsley
4 ounces bulk sausage or sausage meat
    removed from the casings
3 garlic cloves, crushed

Sauce
1 cup finely chopped gherkin pickles
¼ cup extra virgin olive oil
1 tablespoon Dijon mustard

one Add the stock to a large saucepan along with the water, bouquet garni, peppercorns, bacon, garlic, and all the vegetables, except the potatoes and cabbage, and season with salt and pepper. Bring to a gentle simmer.

Two Meanwhile, put all the stuffing ingredients in a bowl and mix thoroughly. Season the cavity of the chicken with salt and pepper. Spoon in the stuffing and truss the chicken closed with string. Place the chicken in the pan, cover, and simmer gently for 1½ hours. Add the cabbage and potatoes, bring back to a boil, and simmer for another 20 minutes.

three Combine all the sauce ingredients in a bowl and mix well. Check that the chicken is cooked all the way through—the juices will run clear when the tip of a sharp knife is inserted into the thickest part of the meat. Remove the chicken from the pan, wrap in aluminum foil, and let rest. Carve the chicken and serve with the vegetables, broth (removing the bouquet garni), and sauce.

Fricassée de volaille

Chicken Stew

❖ Serves 4
❖ Prepared in
  20–25 minutes
❖ Cooks in 35–40 minutes

1 tablespoon all-purpose flour
4 skinless, boneless chicken
   breasts, about 5 ounces each,
   trimmed of all visible fat and
   cut into ¾-inch cubes
1 tablespoon sunflower or
   vegetable oil
8 pearl onions
2 garlic cloves, crushed
1 cup chicken stock
2 carrots, diced
2 celery stalks, diced
1½ cups frozen peas
1 yellow bell pepper, seeded
   and diced
1½ cups sliced white button
   mushrooms
½ cup low-fat plain yogurt
3 tablespoons chopped fresh
   flat-leaf parsley
salt and white pepper

one

two

three

one Spread out the flour on a dish and season with salt and pepper. Add the chicken and, using your hands, coat in the flour.

two Heat the oil in a large casserole dish. Add the onions and garlic and cook over low heat, stirring occasionally, for 5 minutes. Add the chicken and cook, stirring, for 10 minutes, or until just beginning to brown.

three Gradually stir in the stock, then add the carrots, celery, and peas. Bring to a boil, then reduce the heat, cover, and simmer for 5 minutes. Add the yellow bell pepper and mushrooms, cover, and simmer for an additional 10 minutes, until the chicken is cooked through. Using a knife, cut into a piece of chicken to make sure the center is no longer pink.

four Stir in the yogurt and chopped parsley and season with salt and pepper. Cook for 1–2 minutes, or until heated through, then serve immediately.

Coq au vin
Chicken in Wine

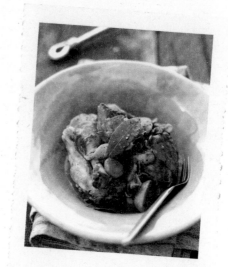

❖ **Serves 4**
❖ **Prepared in 15–20 minutes**
❖ **Cooks in 1½ hours**

4 tablespoons salted butter

2 tablespoons olive oil

4 pounds skinless, boneless chicken breasts

4 ounces rindless smoked bacon, cut into strips

4 ounces pearl onions

4 ounces cremini mushrooms, halved

2 garlic cloves, finely chopped

2 tablespoons brandy

1 cup red wine

1¼ cups chicken stock

1 bouquet garni of 2 thyme sprigs, 2 parsley
   sprigs, and 3 bay leaves, tied with string

2 tablespoons all-purpose flour

salt and pepper

bay leaves, to garnish (optional)

one Melt half of the butter with the olive oil in a large casserole dish. Add the chicken and cook over medium heat, stirring, for 8–10 minutes, or until golden brown all over. Add the bacon, onions, mushrooms, and garlic.

Two Pour in the brandy and set alight with a match. When the flames die down, add the wine, stock, and bouquet garni and season with salt and pepper. Bring to a boil, reduce the heat, and simmer gently for 1 hour, or until the chicken breasts are cooked through. Using a knife, cut into a breast to make sure the center is no longer pink. Transfer the chicken to a large plate, using a slotted spoon, and keep warm. Discard the bouquet garni.

three Meanwhile, mash the remaining butter with the flour in a bowl to make a paste. Slowly stir the butter-and-flour paste into the casserole dish. Bring to a boil, return the chicken to the dish, and serve immediately, garnished with bay leaves (for decoration only).

Coq au Riesling
Chicken in Riesling

✤ Serves 4–6
✤ Prepared in 10 minutes
✤ Cooks in 40–45 minutes

3½-pound chicken, cut into
   8 pieces
2 tablespoons all-purpose
   flour, seasoned with salt
   and pepper
4 tablespoons salted butter,
   plus extra for the pasta
1 tablespoon sunflower oil,
   plus extra if needed
4 shallots, finely chopped
1 pound cremini mushrooms,
   sliced
2 tablespoons brandy
1¼ cups Riesling wine or other
   white wine
2 carrots, thinly sliced
½ cup crème fraîche or
   heavy cream
salt and pepper
ribbon pasta, such as
   pappardelle or tagliatelle,
   to serve

one

three

four

one Coat the chicken pieces with the seasoned flour, shaking off any excess, and set aside. Melt 2 tablespoons of the butter with the oil in a large casserole dish over medium heat. Add the chicken pieces to the dish and sauté for 3–5 minutes, or until golden brown, removing each piece when it is browned and adding extra oil, if necessary. Wipe out the casserole dish.

Two Melt the remaining butter in the dish. Add the shallots and sauté, stirring, for 2–3 minutes, or until soft. Add the mushrooms and a pinch of salt and continue sautéing until the liquid they release is absorbed. Return the chicken to the casserole dish. Light the brandy in a ladle and pour over the chicken.

three When the flames die down, add the wine and carrots and enough water to cover all the ingredients. Bring to a boil, then reduce the heat to low and simmer for 20–25 minutes, or until the chicken is cooked all the way through and the juices run clear when the tip of a sharp knife is inserted into the thickest part of the meat.

four Meanwhile, preheat the oven to 225°F. Bring a saucepan of lightly salted water to a boil, add the pasta, bring back to a boil, and cook for 8–10 minutes, or according to the package directions, until tender but still firm to the bite. Drain well, toss with butter, and keep warm in the preheated oven. Using tongs and a slotted spoon, transfer the chicken and the vegetables to a serving platter and keep warm in the oven. Skim any fat off the cooking juices, stir in the crème fraîche, and bring to a boil, stirring, for 2–3 minutes to reduce. Taste and adjust the seasoning, if necessary, then pour the sauce over the chicken and vegetables. Serve immediately with pasta.

Meat, Poultry & Game

Confit de canard

Duck Confit

* ❖ Serves 4
* ❖ Prepared in 5 minutes, plus chilling and maturing
* ❖ Cooks in 3–4 hours

4 duck legs, about 10 ounces each
¼ cup coarse sea salt
1 teaspoon pepper
6 fresh thyme sprigs, chopped
4 fresh rosemary sprigs, chopped
2 bay leaves
5–6 cups duck fat, goose fat, or lard, plus extra, if necessary
sautéed potatoes and green salad, to serve

one Select one or two airtight, heatproof nonmetallic containers to store the duck legs in, and prepare this recipe at least eight days before you plan to use the duck legs. Rub each duck leg with the salt, then put them in the container or containers. Sprinkle with the pepper, thyme, and rosemary and tuck in the bay leaves. Cover tightly and refrigerate for at least 24 hours or for up to 48 hours.

Two To cook, preheat the oven to 250°F. Wipe the duck legs and discard the accumulated moisture and flavorings. Place the duck legs in a large casserole dish. Add the fat and heat until it melts. Cover the dish and transfer it to the oven for 3–4 hours, or until the duck legs have rendered their fat and are tender.

Three Remove the legs and set aside. Strain the fat through a fine strainer. Pour a layer of the fat in the bottom of the container or containers and let set. Add the duck legs and pour enough fat over them to cover by at least 1 inch.

four Let the duck legs and fat cool, then cover and refrigerate for at least 1 week before using. When ready to use, place the container in simmering water to melt the fat. At this point the duck legs can be used in other recipes or cooked to serve with a salad. To cook, heat 2 tablespoons of the fat in a skillet over medium–high heat. Sauté the duck legs, skin side down, for 4–5 minutes, or until the skin browns. Turn them over and sauté on the other side for an additional 2 minutes. Serve immediately, with the potatoes and salad.

Magret de canard
Duck Breasts with Plum Sauce

✤ Serves 4
✤ Prepared in
   10–15 minutes
✤ Cooks in 25–30 minutes

1 tablespoon duck fat or
   sunflower oil
4 duck breasts, about 12 ounces
   each, finely scored through
   the skin to the fat
cooked green beans, to serve

Plum sauce
1 tablespoon sunflower oil
1 shallot, finely chopped
1½ tablespoons firmly packed
   light brown sugar, plus extra,
   if needed
½ teaspoon ground ginger
4 plums, pitted and coarsely
   chopped
¼ cup dry white wine
1 teaspoon orange juice,
   plus extra, if needed
salt and pepper

one Preheat the oven to 400°F. To make the sauce, heat the oil in a skillet over high heat. Add the shallot and cook until soft. Stir in the sugar and ginger, add the plums, and season with salt and pepper. Stir until the sugar is dissolved and is just beginning to caramelize. Stir in the wine and orange juice immediately and bring to a boil, stirring. Reduce the heat to low and let simmer until the plums are tender and beginning to fall apart and the liquid is reduced. Taste and adjust the seasoning with salt and pepper, if needed. Add extra sugar or orange juice depending on the tartness or sweetness of the plums. Cover the sauce and set aside until required.

Two Meanwhile, melt the duck fat in a large casserole dish wide enough to hold all the breasts in a single layer, or use a large skillet with an ovenproof handle. Add the duck breasts, skin side down, and cook for 3–5 minutes, or until golden brown. Turn the duck breasts skin side up and put them in the oven for 10 minutes for medium–rare and up to 15 minutes for well done. Transfer the duck breasts to a cutting board, cover, and let rest for 5 minutes.

Three Thinly slice the duck breasts diagonally and transfer to warm plates. Add any accumulated juices to the sauce and quickly return the sauce to a boil to reheat. Serve immediately, with the sauce spooned over the duck breasts and the green beans alongside.

one

Two

Three

BRASSERIE DE LA CANCHE

chapter three
Fish & Seafood

Sole meunière

Sole à la florentine

Grand aïoli

Tartare de saumon

Truite pochée

Steaks de thon

Loup de mer frit

Bouillinade

Soufflé au crabe

Brochettes de crevettes

Salade de homard

Crevettes à la grecque

Bouillabaisse

Moules au cidre

Moules marinières

Molusques au safran

Fruits de mer

Coquilles Saint-Jacques

Sole meunière

Butter-Fried Sole

* ❖ Serves 2
* ❖ Prepared in 15–20 minutes
* ❖ Cooks in 15–20 minutes

4 sole fillets, about 6 ounces each, skinned
½ cup whole milk
¼ cup all-purpose flour

6 tablespoons salted butter
juice of ½ lemon
salt and pepper
chopped fresh flat-leaf parsley, to garnish
cooked asparagus and lemon
 wedges, to serve

one Rinse the fish under cold, running water and pat dry with paper towels. Pour the milk into a flat dish at least as large as the fillets and put the flour on a plate. Season each fillet on both sides with salt and pepper.

Two Working with one fillet at a time, pull it quickly through the milk, then put it in the flour, turn once to coat all over, and shake off any excess flour. Continue until all the fillets are prepared.

Three Melt half of the butter in a sauté pan or skillet large enough to hold the fillets in a single layer, over medium–high heat. Add the fillets to the pan, skinned side down, and cook for 2 minutes.

four Turn over the fillets and cook for 2–3 minutes, or until the flesh flakes easily. Transfer to warm serving plates, skinned side up, and set aside.

five Reduce the heat to medium and melt the remaining butter in the pan. When it stops foaming, add the lemon juice and stir, scraping the sediment from the bottom of the pan. Spoon the butter mixture over the fish and garnish with parsley. Serve with asparagus and lemon wedges.

Sole à la florentine
Sole with Mornay Sauce

❖ Serves 4
❖ Prepared in 5 minutes
❖ Cooks in 40 minutes

1 lemon, thinly sliced
1 onion, thinly sliced
1 bay leaf
4 lemon sole fillets, each about
   6 ounces, skinned
2 tablespoons salted butter,
   plus extra for greasing
1¼ pounds fresh spinach,
   thick stems removed
salt and pepper

Mornay sauce
2 tablespoons salted butter
¼ cup all-purpose flour
2 cups boiling whole milk
3 egg yolks beaten with
   3 tablespoons heavy cream
   in a small heatproof bowl
1¼ cups shredded Gruyère
   cheese or Swiss cheese
freshly grated nutmeg, to taste
salt and white pepper

two

four

four

one To make the sauce, melt the butter in a heavy saucepan. Remove the pan from the heat and stir in the flour, using a small whisk or wooden spoon. Return the pan to the heat and cook over medium heat, stirring continuously, for 2 minutes.

two Whisk in the milk and bring to a boil, whisking. As soon as it boils, reduce the heat to low and simmer for 20 minutes, stirring occasionally, or until thick and smooth. Strain through a fine strainer if there are any lumps. Return the sauce to the pan, if necessary, and bring back to a boil. Stir 2 tablespoons of the boiling sauce into the egg mixture, then add the mixture to the pan. Reduce the heat and let bubble for 1 minute. Remove the pan from the heat and stir in 1 cup of the cheese. Season to taste with nutmeg, salt, and white pepper. Cover and set aside.

three Meanwhile, preheat the broiler to high and grease a large ovenproof dish. Put the lemon, onion, bay leaf, and ¼ teaspoon of salt in a large skillet with 2 inches water and bring to a boil. Reduce the heat to low, add the sole, and poach for 4–6 minutes, until the flesh flakes easily. Remove the sole and set aside; discard the flavorings.

four Melt the butter in a large saucepan over medium–high heat. Rinse the spinach and shake dry. Add the spinach with only the water clinging to its leaves, pushing it down with a wooden spoon, if necessary. Season with salt and pepper and simmer for 3–4 minutes, or until wilted. Drain the spinach in a strainer, pushing out any excess water. Arrange the spinach in the prepared dish and top with the sole. Pour the sauce over the fish and sprinkle with the remaining cheese. Put the dish under the preheated broiler, about 4 inches from the heat, and broil for 3–5 minutes, or until golden and bubbling. Serve immediately.

Grand aïoli

Provençal Salmon & Vegetables

❖ Serves 8
❖ Prepared in 25–30 minutes
❖ Cooks in 45 minutes

3¼ pounds salmon, cod, or
  pollock fillets, skinned
1 pound new potatoes
3½ cups trimmed green beans
1 pound small or baby
  carrots
1 pound baby zucchini
1 large head of cauliflower,
  cut into florets

1 large head of broccoli,
  cut into florets
4 tomatoes, quartered

Court bouillon
9 cups water
1 cup white wine
1 carrot, sliced
1 celery stalk, sliced
½ onion, sliced
½ teaspoon black peppercorns
2 teaspoons salt
1 bay leaf

Aioli
4 garlic cloves, chopped
2 egg yolks
1 teaspoon Dijon mustard
1 cup extra virgin olive oil
1¼ cups sunflower oil
1 tablespoon lemon juice
¼ cup cold water
salt and pepper

one Place all the court bouillon ingredients in a large saucepan or fish poacher. Place over low heat and simmer for 15 minutes, then add the salmon, cod, or pollock. When it returns to a simmer, reduce the heat to as low as possible so the liquid just shudders occasionally. Poach, covered, for 5 minutes, then remove the fish, using a spatula, and set aside to cool. Keep warm.

Two To make the aioli, combine the garlic, egg yolks, and mustard in a food processor. Process, slowly pouring in the oils one after the other in a slow, regular trickle—they will eventually thicken into a firm, thick, fluffy mayonnaise. Add the lemon juice and cold water, season generously, and blend briefly. Place in small serving bowls.

three Bring a large saucepan of lightly salted water to a boil, add the potatoes, and cook for 10–15 minutes, or until just tender. Bring another saucepan of water to a boil and steam the remaining vegetables, except the tomatoes, for 2–4 minutes each. Lightly blanch tomatoes for a minute or two, just enough so that they retain a good crunch. Put the fish in the middle of a large serving platter and surround it with all the vegetables. Serve with the bowls of aioli.

tartare de saumon

Salmon Tartare

✤ Serves 4
✤ Prepared in
   25–30 minutes,
   plus chilling
✤ No cooking

1 pound salmon fillet, skinned
2 tablespoons sea salt
1 tablespoon sugar
2 tablespoons chopped
   fresh dill
1 tablespoon chopped
   fresh tarragon
1 teaspoon Dijon mustard
juice of 1 lemon
salt and pepper
snipped fresh dill and chives,
   to garnish

Topping
1¾ cups cream cheese
1 tablespoon chopped fresh
   chives
pinch of paprika

one

two

three

one Put the salmon into a shallow ovenproof dish. Combine the sea salt, sugar, and dill, then rub the mixture into the fish until well coated. Season with plenty of pepper. Cover with plastic wrap and refrigerate for at least 48 hours, turning the salmon once.

two When ready to serve, put the chopped tarragon into a mixing bowl with the mustard and lemon juice. Season well. Remove the salmon from the refrigerator, chop it into small pieces, then add to the bowl. Stir until the salmon is well coated.

three To make the topping, put the cream cheese, chives, and paprika into a separate bowl and mix well. Place a 4-inch steel cooking ring or round pastry cutter on each of four small serving plates. Divide the salmon between the four steel rings so that each ring is filled halfway. Level the surface of each one, then top with the cream cheese mixture. Smooth the surfaces, then carefully remove the steel rings. Garnish with fresh dill and chives and serve immediately.

Truite pochée
Poached Trout

* ✤ Serves 4
* ✤ Prepared in 10–15 minutes
* ✤ Cooks in 15 minutes

4 whole rainbow trout, gutted and fins
   removed, with head left on or removed
about 5 cups Court Bouillon (see page 96)
lemon wedges and fresh tarragon sprigs,
   to garnish

Beurre blanc
3 tablespoons finely chopped shallots
2 bay leaves
6 peppercorns, crushed
3 tablespoons white wine
3 tablespoons white wine vinegar
1½ tablespoons heavy cream
1½ sticks salted butter, diced
2 teaspoons chopped fresh tarragon
salt and pepper

one Rinse the trout inside and out under cold running water and pat dry
with paper towels. To make the beurre blanc, put the shallots, bay leaves,
peppercorns, wine, and vinegar in a saucepan and boil until reduced to
1 tablespoon. Strain the mixture, then return to the saucepan. Stir in the cream,
bring to a boil, then reduce the heat. Whisk in the butter gradually, and stir in
the tarragon. Season with salt and pepper and place in serving bowls.

Two Put the trout in a skillet large enough to hold them side by side. Pour
over enough court bouillon to cover and bring to a boil. Reduce the heat to low
immediately and let simmer for 8–10 minutes, or until the flesh flakes easily.

Three Remove the fish from the liquid and pat dry. The fish can now be
served whole or skinned and filleted. Transfer to warm plates, garnish with the
lemon wedges and tarragon sprigs, and serve with the beurre blanc.

Steaks de Thon

Tuna Steaks

* Serves 4
* Prepared in 10 minutes, plus chilling
* Cooks in 3–4½ minutes

4 tuna steaks, each about
  1½ inches thick, at room
  temperature
olive oil, for brushing
salt and pepper
mixed salad greens, to serve

Mediterranean butter
1 garlic clove, finely chopped
1 stick salted butter, softened
2 tablespoons chopped
  fresh dill
4 ripe black olives in brine,
  drained, pitted and
  finely chopped
2 anchovy fillets in oil, drained
  and finely chopped
2 sun-dried tomatoes in oil,
  drained and finely chopped
finely grated rind of 1 lemon
pinch of cayenne pepper,
  or to taste
salt and pepper

one

Two

Three

one At least 3 hours before you plan to cook, make the butter. Put the garlic clove on a cutting board and sprinkle with salt. Use the flat side of a knife to crush and scrape the garlic until a paste forms. Beat together the garlic, butter, dill, olives, anchovies, sun-dried tomatoes, lemon rind, and cayenne pepper in a bowl until all the ingredients are mixed. Season with salt and pepper.

Two Scrape the butter mixture onto a piece of wax paper and roll into a short log about 1 inch thick. Twist the ends of the paper to make a compact shape, then cut off any excess paper from one end. Stand the butter log upright in a glass and chill for at least 3 hours.

Three Heat a large, ridged grill pan over high heat. Brush the tuna with oil and season with salt and pepper on both sides. Place the tuna steaks in the pan and grill for 2 minutes. Brush the tuna with a little more oil, turn the steaks over, and continue cooking for an additional 1 minute for medium–rare or up to 2½ minutes for well done. Transfer the tuna steaks to plates and top each with a slice of the chilled butter. Serve immediately, with mixed salad greens.

Loup de mer frit
Pan-Fried Sea Bass

❖ Serves 4
❖ Prepared in 20–25 minutes
❖ Cooks in 35–40 minutes

7 russet potatoes (1¾ pounds), peeled and cut
   into chunks
6 whole garlic cloves, unpeeled
1 cup whole milk
½ cup heavy cream
4 tablespoons salted butter, diced
4 sea bass fillets, about 6 ounces,
   scaled but not skinned
3 tablespoons olive oil
salt and pepper
peas and lemon wedges, to serve

one Fill a large saucepan with cold water, add some salt and the potatoes, and bring to a boil. Simmer for 10–15 minutes, or until tender, then drain and return to the pan. Heat and stir for an additional 2 minutes to dry them out. Mash them using a potato ricer (a potato masher won't make them smooth enough) and set aside in the warm pan.

Two Bring a small saucepan of water to a boil, add the garlic, and blanch for 2 minutes, then drain and run under a little cold water. Peel off the skins and mash the garlic, using a garlic crusher or the back of a spoon. Mix this into the potatoes. Put the milk in a saucepan and heat until hot but not boiling, then stir it into the potatoes, along with the cream. Heat over low heat for about 5 minutes, adding the butter a cube at a time. The potatoes should have a smooth consistency like a thick mayonnaise. Cover and keep warm.

Three Carefully score the skin of the fish with a few diagonal cuts, being careful not to cut the flesh. Season with salt and pepper. Pour the oil into a large skillet and place over medium–high heat until shimmering. Cook the fillets, skin side down, for 4 minutes. Check that the skin is crispy, then turn carefully and cook on the other side for just 1 minute. Spread some potato in the center of four warm plates and place a fish fillet on top, skin side up. Serve with peas and lemon wedges.

Bouillinade

Fish & Potato Casserole

❖ Serves 4
❖ Prepared in 5 minutes
❖ Cooks in 30–45 minutes

1½ tablespoons olive oil, plus
   extra for brushing
1 onion, finely chopped
3 large garlic cloves,
   2 chopped and 1 halved
1 tablespoon fennel seeds
½ teaspoon crushed red
   pepper, or to taste
pinch of saffron threads
1 (14½-ounce) can diced
   tomatoes
½ cup fish stock or water
2 bay leaves
4 Yukon gold or white round
   potatoes, thinly sliced
2 pounds mixed fish, such
   as hake, monkfish, and
   red snapper, skinned and
   cut into chunks
2 red bell peppers, seeded
   and sliced
2 tablespoons chopped fresh
   flat-leaf parsley
salt and pepper

one Preheat the oven to 350°F.

Two Heat the oil in a saucepan over medium heat. Add the onion and sauté, stirring, for 2 minutes. Add the chopped garlic, fennel seeds, crushed red pepper, and saffron and continue sautéing for an additional 1 minute, or until the onion is soft. Add the tomatoes, stock, and bay leaves and season with salt and pepper. Cover and bring to a boil, then reduce the heat to low and simmer for 10 minutes. Taste and adjust the seasoning, if necessary.

three Meanwhile, rub the garlic halves all over a 1½-quart ovenproof dish, pressing down firmly, then set aside the dish, discarding the garlic. Bring a large saucepan of lightly salted water to a boil, add the potatoes, bring back to a boil, and cook for 8–10 minutes, or until they are starting to soften but still hold their shape. Drain well, pat dry, and set aside.

four Place the prepared dish on a baking sheet and arrange half the potatoes in a layer at the bottom of the dish. Place the fish and red bell peppers on top. Spoon the tomato sauce over the fish, sprinkle with the parsley, and shake the dish slightly. Arrange the remaining potatoes on top to cover all the other ingredients and lightly brush with oil. Bake in the preheated oven for 20–25 minutes, or until the fish and potatoes are tender when pierced with the tines of a fork. Serve immediately.

Two

three

four

Soufflé au crabe
Crab Soufflé

❖ Serves 4
❖ Prepared in 20–25 minutes
❖ Cooks in 50–55 minutes

1 clove
2 small shallots, 1 whole, 1 finely chopped
1 cup whole milk
6 black peppercorns
1 bay leaf
2 tablespoons salted butter, plus extra for greasing

3 tablespoons all-purpose flour, plus extra for dusting
4 eggs, whites and yolks separated into separate bowls
½ teaspoon cayenne pepper
8 ounces cooked crabmeat

one Preheat the oven to 400°F. Carefully grease a deep 1-quart soufflé dish, then dust with flour, turning the dish around so that it is completely coated. Discard any excess. Push the clove into the whole shallot and place in a small saucepan with the milk, peppercorns, and bay leaf. Heat until just simmering, then remove from the heat and let cool. Strain, reserving the milk and discarding the solids.

Two Place a saucepan over low heat and add the butter and the chopped shallot. Cook for about 5 minutes, or until the shallot is soft. Add the flour and cook for 3 minutes, stirring, to make a roux. Remove from the heat and add the reserved milk a little at a time, stirring continuously so that it doesn't become lumpy. Add the egg yolks and cayenne pepper and beat them in thoroughly with a whisk. Add the crabmeat and warm through again, but don't boil. Pour into a mixing bowl.

three In a clean, grease-free bowl, whisk the egg whites until soft peaks form. Add to the crab mixture one-quarter at a time, gently folding through. Spoon into the prepared soufflé dish, place in the preheated oven, and bake for 25–30 minutes, or until golden on top. Do not open the oven door until it's cooked. Serve immediately.

Brochettes de crevettes
Shrimp Kabobs

❖ Serves 4
❖ Prepared in 10 minutes,
  plus infusing
❖ Cooks in 10–15 minutes

⅔ cup olive oil
finely grated zest of 1 lemon
pinch of cayenne pepper,
  or to taste
1 bunch fresh thyme sprigs,
  tied together
2 red bell peppers, seeded
  and cut into 1-inch pieces
20 jumbo shrimp, peeled
  and deveined
salt and pepper
lemon wedges and thyme
  sprigs, to serve

one

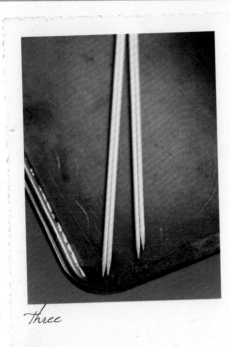
three

three

one At least 1 hour before cooking, put the oil in a shallow bowl with the lemon zest and cayenne pepper and season with salt and pepper. Position the thyme sprigs so the leaves are submerged in the oil and set aside for the flavors to steep the oil.

Two Meanwhile, light a barbecue grill and let stand until the coals turn gray, or preheat the broiler to high and position the broiler rack about 4 inches from the heat. If using wooden skewers, presoak four in a bowl of water. Bring a small saucepan of water to a boil, add the bell pepper pieces, and blanch for 1–2 minutes, or until just tender. Drain well and rinse immediately under cold water. Set aside.

three When ready to cook, drain the wooden skewers, if using. Use the thyme sprigs to brush four long metal or wooden skewers with the flavored oil. Arrange five shrimp and six bell pepper pieces on each skewer, alternating the pieces and starting and ending with bell pepper, and brush with the flavored oil on both sides.

four Place the skewers on the grill rack or under the broiler and cook for 3 minutes. Turn them over, brush again with the oil, and cook for an additional 2–3 minutes, or until the shrimp turn pink and the bell peppers are lightly charred and tender. Serve immediately with lemon wedges and thyme sprigs.

Salade de homard
Lobster Salad

❖ Serves 4
❖ Prepared in 25–30 minutes, plus freezing
❖ Cooks in 15–20 minutes

2 live lobsters, around 1½ pounds, or 1 pound cooked fresh lobster meat
1 cucumber
1 lettuce
4 hard-boiled eggs, halved
salt and pepper
cooked new potatoes, to serve

Mayonnaise
2 egg yolks
1 teaspoon Dijon mustard
½ cup extra virgin olive oil
⅔ cup sunflower oil
1 tablespoon lemon juice
¼ cup cold water
small handful of fresh flat-leaf parsley, finely chopped
small handful of fresh dill, finely chopped
small handful of fresh chervil leaves (optional), finely chopped
salt and pepper

one If using fresh lobsters, put them into the freezer for 2 hours to kill them. Bring a large saucepan of heavily salted water to a boil and add the lobsters. Bring back to a boil and cook for 15 minutes. Remove from the heat, drain, and let cool.

two To make the mayonnaise, combine the egg yolks and mustard in a food processor. Turn the processor on and, with the motor running, pour in the olive oil and then the sunflower oil in a slow, regular trickle, until the mixture has a good, thick consistency. Add the lemon juice and water, season with salt and pepper, and process again. Fold the herbs through, then place in a bowl and refrigerate.

three Peel, halve, and seed the cucumber. Cut into thin slivers using a vegetable peeler. Cut the lobster in half lengthwise, remove the dark vein that runs along the back of the tail, then remove the stomach sac that sits behind the mouth. Crack the claws with the back of a heavy knife.

four Lay a bed of lettuce on each plate, sprinkle some cucumber over the lettuce, then lay two egg halves and the lobster half or meat on top. Season with salt and pepper, add a spoonful of the herby mayonnaise, and serve with potatoes.

Crevettes à la grecque

Shrimp in Mediterranean Sauce

✤ Serves 4
✤ Prepared in
   12–15 minutes, plus
   cooling and chilling
✤ Cooks in 30 minutes

½ cup dry white wine
½ cup water
⅓ cup olive oil
2 large garlic cloves,
   thinly sliced
1 small red onion,
   finely chopped
thinly pared zest of
   1 large lemon
2 tablespoons lemon juice
1 tablespoon coriander seeds,
   toasted and lightly crushed
½ tablespoon black or pink
   peppercorns, lightly crushed
pinch of crushed red pepper,
   or to taste
20 jumbo shrimp, peeled
   and deveined
salt and pepper
chopped fresh flat-leaf parsley,
   dill, or cilantro, to garnish
sliced baguette, to serve

one

two

three

one Put the wine, water, oil, garlic, onion, lemon zest and juice, coriander seeds, peppercorns, and crushed red pepper into a saucepan. Cover and bring to a boil over high heat, then reduce the heat and simmer for 20 minutes.

two Add the shrimp to the liquid and simmer for 2–3 minutes, or until they turn pink. Use a slotted spoon to remove the shrimp from the liquid immediately and transfer them to a deep bowl.

three Bring the poaching liquid back to a boil, uncovered, and boil for 5 minutes, or until reduced by half. Let cool to lukewarm, then pour the liquid over the shrimp. Season the shrimp with salt and pepper and let cool completely. Cover the bowl with plastic wrap and chill for at least 4 hours.

four When ready to serve, garnish with parsley and serve chilled, with plenty of sliced baguette for mopping up the juices.

Bouillabaisse

Seafood Stew

+ Serves 8
+ Prepared in 20–25 minutes
+ Cooks in 50–55 minutes

2¼ pounds of at least 4 different firm white
   fish fillets, such as red snapper, sea bass,
   rockfish, or monkfish, scaled and cleaned,
   but not skinned
½ cup olive oil
2 onions, finely chopped
1 fennel bulb, finely chopped
4 garlic cloves, crushed
3 (14½-ounce) cans
   diced tomatoes
6½ cups fish stock
pinch of saffron strands
grated zest of 1 orange

bouquet garni of 2 thyme sprigs, 2 parsley
   sprigs, and 2 bay leaves, tied with string
1 pound mussels, scrubbed and debearded
1 pound cooked shrimp, shell on
salt and pepper
baguette, to serve

one Carefully pin bone the fish, then cut the fillets into bite-size pieces. Heat the olive oil in a large skillet or wide saucepan with a lid and gently sauté the onion and fennel for about 15 minutes, or until soft. Add the garlic and sauté for 2 minutes, then add the tomatoes and simmer for 2 minutes. Add the stock, saffron, orange zest, and bouquet garni and bring to a boil. Simmer, uncovered, for 15 minutes.

two Discard any mussels with broken shells and any that refuse to close when tapped. Add the fish pieces, mussels, and shrimp and cover the skillet. Simmer for an additional 5–10 minutes, or until the mussels have opened. Discard any that remain closed. Season with salt and pepper.

three Serve immediately with some crusty baguette.

Moules au cidre

Mussels in Cider

✤ **Serves 4**
✤ **Prepared in 15 minutes**
✤ **Cooks in 25 minutes**

4½ pounds live mussels,
   scrubbed and debearded
1¼ cups hard dry cider
6 shallots, finely chopped
⅓ cup heavy cream
pepper
baguette, to serve

two

three

four

one Discard any mussels with broken shells or any that refuse to close when tapped.

Two Pour the cider into a large casserole dish, add the shallots, and season with pepper. Bring to a boil and cook for 2 minutes.

Three Add the mussels, cover with a tight-fitting lid, and cook over high heat, shaking the casserole dish occasionally, for about 5 minutes, or until the shells have opened. Remove the mussels with a slotted spoon, discarding any that remain closed, and keep warm.

four Strain the cooking liquid through a cheesecloth-lined strainer into a saucepan. Bring to a boil and cook for 8–10 minutes, or until reduced by about half. Stir in the cream and add the mussels. Cook for 1 minute to reheat the shellfish, then serve immediately with baguette.

Moules marinières
Mussels in Wine

* ❧ Serves 4
* ❧ Prepared in 10–15 minutes
* ❧ Cooks in 8–10 minutes

4½ pounds mussels, scrubbed and debearded
1¼ cups dry white wine
6 shallots, finely chopped
bouquet garni of 2 thyme sprigs, 2 parsley
  sprigs, and 2 bay leaves, tied with string
pepper
fresh flat-leaf parsley sprigs,
  to garnish
baguette, to serve

one Discard any mussels with broken shells and any that refuse to close when tapped.

Two Pour the wine into a large, heavy saucepan, add the shallots and bouquet garni, and season with pepper. Bring to a boil over medium heat, add the mussels, and cover tightly. Cook, shaking the saucepan occasionally, for 3–4 minutes, or until the mussels have opened. Remove and discard the bouquet garni and any mussels that remain closed.

three Using a slotted spoon, divide the mussels among individual serving dishes. Tilt the saucepan to let any sand settle, then spoon the cooking liquid over the mussels. Garnish with parsley sprigs and serve immediately with baguette.

Molusques au safran
Shellfish in Saffron Sauce

* ✤ Serves 4
* ✤ Prepared in 25–30 minutes
* ✤ Cooks in 20–25 minutes

24 large shrimp, peeled and deveined, heads and shells reserved

1⅔ cups water

1 cup white vermouth

1 fennel bulb, sliced

1 leek, chopped

2 garlic cloves, crushed

large pinch of saffron threads

2 pounds live mussels, scrubbed and debearded

2 pounds live clams, scrubbed

2 tablespoons salted butter

1 shallot, finely chopped

1 cup crème fraîche

salt and white pepper

4 Garlic Toasts (see page 36)

chopped fresh flat-leaf parsley, to garnish

Two

Two

Three

one Put the shrimp shells, water, vermouth, fennel, leek, garlic, saffron, and a pinch of salt into a saucepan. Cover and bring to a boil, then reduce the heat and simmer for 15 minutes to concentrate the flavors. Strain the stock and set aside. Meanwhile, discard any mussels or clams with broken shells and any that refuse to close when tapped.

Two Melt the butter in a large sauté pan or skillet. Add the shallot and cook, stirring, for 2–3 minutes, or until soft. Stir in 1 cup of the reserved stock and bring to a boil. Reduce the heat to low, add the shrimp, and simmer for 2–3 minutes, or until they turn pink. Using a slotted spoon, remove the shrimp from the liquid immediately and keep warm. Add the mussels and clams to the pan, cover, and cook, shaking the pan, for 2–5 minutes, or until all the mussels and clams open. Use tongs or a slotted spoon to remove the open mussels and clams, discarding any that remain closed. When the mussels and clams are cool enough to handle, remove the top shells and discard, then set the mussels and clams aside with the shrimp and keep warm.

Three Stir the crème fraîche and the remaining stock into the pan. Return the liquid to a boil and boil for 5–8 minutes, or until reduced to about 1½ cups. Taste and adjust the seasoning, if necessary. Arrange the garlic toasts in the bottom of four bowls. Top with the shrimp, mussels, and clams and ladle the saffron sauce over the seafood. Garnish with parsley and serve immediately.

123

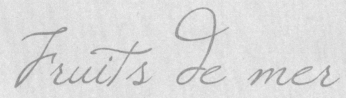

Fruits de mer

Seafood in the Shell

❖ Serves 8
❖ Prepared in 10 minutes
❖ No cooking

large bag of ice cubes
a maximum of 1½ pounds mixed
   shellfish per person, such as from the
   following list, prepared and cooked:
   lobster
   crab
   oysters
   large shrimp in their shells
   mussels
   clams
   razor clams

   cockles or baby clams
   whelks

Shallot vinegar
1 shallot
¼ cup red wine vinegar

To serve
baguette, sliced
mayonnaise
lemon wedges
Tabasco sauce

one Create a bed of crushed ice by taking a few handfuls of ice cubes at a time and placing them in an old dish towel. Beat them with a rolling pin, mallet, or hammer until they have been crushed to a coarse, gravelly consistency. Keep in the freezer.

Two To make the shallot vinegar, finely chop the shallot and mix with the vinegar in a small bowl.

three Lay a bed of crushed ice on a large serving plate, then make a centerpiece, using the lobster cut in half and the crab with the shell cracked ready for eating. Discard any oysters, mussels, clams, razor clams, cockles, or welks with broken shells or any that remain closed. The oysters should surround the centerpiece, interspersed with the shrimp (in their whole shells), mussels, and clams, and the other bivalves scattered wherever they can fit (usually served in the shell they are attached to).

four Serve with the shallot vinegar, sliced baguette, mayonnaise in small dishes, lemon wedges, and Tabasco sauce. Put a large bowl on the table for the discarded shells.

Coquilles Saint-Jacques

Scallops with Bread Crumbs

❖ Serves 4
❖ Prepared in
   10–15 minutes
❖ Cooks in 20 minutes

20 large fresh scallops,
  removed from their shells
1¾ sticks salted butter, plus
  extra, if needed
3 slices day-old French bread,
  made into fine bread crumbs
4 garlic cloves, finely chopped
⅓ cup finely chopped fresh
  flat-leaf parsley
salt and pepper
lemon wedges, to serve

one Preheat the oven to 225°F. Use a small knife to remove the dark vein that runs around each scallop, then rinse and pat dry. Season with salt and pepper and set aside.

Two Melt half of the butter in a large sauté pan or skillet over high heat. Add the bread crumbs and garlic, reduce the heat to medium, and sauté, stirring, for 5–6 minutes, or until golden brown. Remove the garlic bread crumbs from the pan and drain well on paper towels, then keep warm in the oven. Wipe out the pan.

three Use two large sauté pans or skillets to cook all the scallops at once without overcrowding the pans. Melt 3½ tablespoons of the butter in each pan over high heat. Reduce the heat to medium, divide the scallops between the two pans in single layers, and cook for 2 minutes.

four Turn the scallops over and continue cooking for an additional 2–3 minutes, or until they are golden and cooked through if you cut one with a knife. Add extra butter to the pans, if necessary.

five Divide the scallops among four warm plates and sprinkle with the bread crumbs and parsley. Serve with lemon wedges for squeezing over the scallops.

Two

Two

four

Vegetable Dishes

Ratatouille

Roasted Vegetables in Sauce

✤ Serves 4
✤ Prepared in 20–25 minutes
✤ Cooks in 1½ hours

3 red bell peppers
1 cup olive oil
1 zucchini, thickly sliced
1 fennel bulb, coarsely chopped
2 large red onions, coarsely sliced

3 white onions, thickly sliced
2 large eggplants, thickly sliced
5 ripe tomatoes, blanched, peeled, cored, and seeded
1 large tablespoon fresh thyme leaves
1 large tablespoon fresh rosemary leaves
1 teaspoon sugar
salt and pepper
crusty bread, to serve (optional)

one Preheat the broiler to high. Put the red bell peppers on the broiler pan and place under the heat until the skin blackens. Turn and broil again, continuing until they are blackened all over. Put them in a bowl and cover with plastic wrap to sweat for 10 minutes, then peel them under cold running water. Cut them open and remove the seeds, then chop the flesh into large chunks.

Two Meanwhile, place a large, heavy saucepan over medium heat and add half of the oil. Add the zucchini and sauté until they begin to brown. Transfer to a large roasting pan and keep warm. Add the fennel and onions to the pan and sauté for 15–20 minutes, until they soften, then add them to the roasting pan. Add the eggplants and some more oil (they will soak up a lot) to the pan and cook until they begin to brown. Add them to the roasting pan, laid flat in a single layer.

three Preheat the oven to 375°F. Add the tomatoes, red bell peppers, thyme, and rosemary to the roasting pan and distribute the vegetables evenly across it. Sprinkle the sugar over everything and gently mix through. There should be one layer of vegetables, not a stew. If you need more room, use two roasting pans. Season with salt and pepper, drizzle with olive oil, and place, uncovered, in the preheated oven for 40–50 minutes, or until they start to brown.

four Refrigerate overnight or serve immediately with crusty bread, if using.

Gratin de courgettes

Zucchini & Cheese Gratin

- ✤ Serves 4–6
- ✤ Prepared in
  25–30 minutes
- ✤ Cooks in 50–55 minutes

4 tablespoons salted butter,
  plus extra for greasing
6 zucchini, sliced
2 tablespoons chopped fresh
  tarragon or a mixture of
  fresh mint, tarragon, and
  flat-leaf parsley
2 cups grated Gruyère cheese
  or Parmesan cheese
½ cup whole milk
½ cup heavy cream
2 eggs, beaten
freshly grated nutmeg
salt and pepper

two

three

four

one Preheat the oven to 350°F. Grease a large ovenproof dish.

two Melt the butter in a large sauté pan or skillet over medium–high heat. Add the zucchini and sauté for 4–6 minutes, turning the slices over occasionally, until browned on both sides. Remove from the pan and drain on paper towels, then season with salt and pepper.

three Spread half of the zucchini over the bottom of the prepared dish. Sprinkle with half of the herbs and one-third of the cheese. Repeat these layers once again.

four Mix together the milk, cream, and eggs in a small bowl and season with nutmeg, salt, and pepper. Pour the mixture over the zucchini, then sprinkle the top with the remaining cheese.

five Bake in the preheated oven for 35–45 minutes, or until it is set in the center and golden brown. Remove from the oven and let stand for 5 minutes before serving straight from the dish.

Tarte à l'oignon
French Onion Tart

❖ Serves 4
❖ Prepared in 20–25 minutes, plus chilling
❖ Cooks in 1¼ hours

Pie dough
1⅔ cups all-purpose flour, plus extra to dust
pinch of salt
1 stick salted butter, plus extra for greasing
1 egg yolk

Filling
5 tablespoons salted butter
4 onions, thinly sliced
2 teaspoons thyme leaves
2 eggs
1 cup heavy cream
½ cup shredded Gruyère cheese
½ teaspoon fresh grated nutmeg
salt and pepper

one Preheat the oven to 350°F and grease an 8-inch loose-bottom tart pan. To make the dough, sift together the flour and salt into a large bowl. Dice the butter, add to the bowl, then rub with your fingers until the mixture resembles fine bread crumbs. Add the egg yolk and just enough water to bind to a soft, but not sticky, dough. Roll into a ball, wrap in plastic wrap, and refrigerate for 15 minutes before using.

Two Roll out the dough on a lightly floured surface. Press the dough into the prepared tart pan, lay a piece of parchment paper on it, fill with pie weights or dried beans, and bake in the preheated oven for 15 minutes. Remove from the oven and increase the oven temperature to 400°F. Remove the paper and weights and bake the pastry shell for an additional 5 minutes. Reduce the oven temperature to 375°F.

three To make the filling, melt the butter in a large, heavy skillet over medium–low heat, add the onions and thyme, and cook gently, stirring frequently, for 15–30 minutes, until lightly browned. Season with salt and pepper, remove from the heat, and let cool for 10 minutes.

four In a large bowl, beat together the eggs and cream. Add the cheese, nutmeg, and cooked onion mixture and stir. Pour the mixture into the pastry shell and bake, uncovered, for 30–40 minutes, or until golden brown. Serve immediately.

Tarte aux Tomates

Tomato Tart

❖ Serves 4
❖ Prepared in
   20–25 minutes
❖ Cooks in 40–45 minutes

Pie dough
2 cups all-purpose flour
pinch of salt
1¼ sticks salted butter
1 tablespoon chopped oregano,
   plus extra to garnish
about ⅓ cup cold water

Filling
2 tablespoons salted butter
1 tablespoon sugar
9 small tomatoes, halved
1 garlic clove, crushed
2 teaspoons white wine vinegar
salt and pepper

one

three

three

one Preheat the oven to 400°F. To make the filling, melt the butter in a heavy saucepan. Add the sugar and stir over high heat until just turning golden brown. Remove from the heat and quickly add the tomatoes, garlic, and white wine vinegar, stirring to coat evenly. Season with salt and pepper.

Two Transfer the tomatoes, cut side down, to a 9-inch cake pan, spreading them evenly.

Three To make the dough, place the flour, salt, butter, and oregano in a food processor and process until the mixture resembles fine bread crumbs. Add just enough water to bind to a soft, but not sticky, dough. Roll out the dough to a 10-inch circle and place it over the tomatoes, tucking in the edges. Pierce with a fork to let out steam.

four Bake in the preheated oven for 25–30 minutes, or until firm and golden. Rest for 2–3 minutes, then run a knife around the edge and invert onto a warm serving plate.

five Sprinkle the tart with chopped oregano, and serve immediately.

137

Tarte aux asperges

Asparagus Tart

❖ Serves 4
❖ Prepared in 20–25 minutes
❖ Cooks in 1¼ hours

1 rolled dough pie crust, chilled
salted butter, for greasing
all-purpose flour, for dusting
1 bunch thin asparagus spears
1 (10-ounce) package fresh spinach leaves
3 extra-large eggs, beaten
⅔ cup heavy cream

1 garlic clove, crushed
10 small cherry tomatoes, halved
handful of chopped fresh basil
¼ cup freshly grated Parmesan cheese
salt and pepper

one Preheat the oven to 375°F. Remove the dough pie crust from the refrigerator at least 15 minutes before use, otherwise it may be brittle and difficult to handle. Grease a 9-inch tart pan with butter, then roll out the dough on a lightly floured surface and line the pan with it. Cut off any excess and prick the bottom with a fork. Cover with a piece of parchment paper, fill with pie weights or dried beans, and bake in the preheated oven for 20–30 minutes, or until lightly browned. Take out of the oven, remove the paper and weights, and let cool slightly. Reduce the oven temperature to 350°F.

Two Meanwhile, bend the asparagus spears until they snap, and discard the tough, woody ends. Bring a large saucepan of water to a boil, add the asparagus, and blanch for 1 minute, then remove and drain. Add the spinach to the boiling water, then remove immediately and drain very well.

three Mix together the eggs, cream, and garlic in a small bowl, and season with salt and pepper. Spread the spinach over the bottom of the pastry shell, add the asparagus and tomatoes, cut side up, sprinkle with the basil, then pour the egg mixture on top. Transfer to the preheated oven and bake for 35 minutes, or until the filling has just set. Sprinkle the Parmesan cheese on top and let cool to room temperature or serve immediately.

Omelette aux fines herbes

Mixed Herb Omelet

* Serves 1
* Prepared in 10 minutes
* Cooks in 15–20 minutes

2 extra-large eggs
2 tablespoons whole milk
3 tablespoons salted butter
leaves from 1 fresh flat-leaf
   parsley sprig, plus extra
   to garnish
1 fresh chervil sprig, chopped,
   plus extra to garnish
2 fresh chives, snipped, plus
   extra to garnish
salt and pepper

one Break the eggs into a bowl. Add the milk, season with salt and pepper, and quickly beat until just blended.

Two Heat an 8-inch omelet pan or skillet over medium-high heat until hot and you can feel the heat rising from the surface. Add 2 tablespoons of the butter and use a fork to rub it over the bottom and around the sides as it melts.

three As soon as the butter stops sizzling, pour in the eggs. Shake the pan back and forth over the heat and use the fork to stir the eggs around the pan in a circular motion. Do not scrape the bottom of the pan.

four As the omelet begins to set, use the fork to push the cooked egg from the edge toward the center, so the remaining uncooked egg comes in contact with the hot bottom of the pan. Continue doing this for 3 minutes, or until the omelet looks set on the bottom but is still slightly runny on top.

five Place the herbs in the center of the omelet. Tilt the pan away from the handle, so the omelet slides toward the edge of the pan. Use the fork to fold the top part of the omelet over the herbs and then fold over the bottom part. Slide the omelet onto a plate, then rub the remaining butter over the top and garnish with the herbs. Omelets are best eaten immediately.

one

four

five

Aumonières de poireaux

Leek Crepes

+ **Makes 8**
+ **Prepared in 20–25 minutes**
+ **Cooks in 35 minutes**

Filling
2 tablespoons unsalted butter
½ tablespoon sunflower oil
2 leeks, finely shredded
freshly grated nutmeg, to taste
1 tablespoon finely snipped fresh chives
3 ounces soft goat cheese, rind removed,
   if necessary, chopped
salt and pepper

Crepes (thin pancakes)
1¼ cups all-purpose flour
pinch of salt
1 cup whole milk
1 extra-large egg
2 tablespoons melted salted butter
salted butter, for cooking

one Preheat the oven to 400°F. To make the filling, melt the butter with the oil in a skillet with a lid over medium–high heat. Add the leeks and stir so that they are well coated. Season with salt and pepper, but remember the cheese might be salty. Add a few gratings of nutmeg, then cover the leeks with a sheet of wet wax paper and put the lid on the skillet. Reduce the heat to low and let the leeks sweat for 5–7 minutes, or until tender but not brown. Stir in the chives, then check the seasoning.

two To make the crepes, sift the flour and salt into a bowl. Add the milk, egg, and melted butter and beat to a smooth batter. Let stand for 15 minutes. Heat the butter in a large skillet. Pour in just enough batter to cover the skillet, swirling to create a thin layer. Cook until the underside is golden, then flip and cook the other side. Repeat with the remaining batter until you have eight crepes.

three Put one crepe on the work surface and put one-eighth of the leeks on the crepe, top with one-eighth of the cheese, then fold the crepe into a square package or simply roll it around the filling. Place the stuffed crepe on a baking sheet, then continue to fill and fold or roll the remaining crepes. Put the baking sheet in the preheated oven and bake for 5 minutes, or until the crepes are hot and the cheese starts to melt. Serve immediately.

Clafoutis au fromage
Cheese Clafoutis

❖ Serves 4–6
❖ Prepared in 15 minutes
❖ Cooks in 50–55 minutes

olive oil, for greasing
3 cups cherry tomatoes
3 ounces goat cheese, rind
   removed, if necessary,
   finely crumbled
2 tablespoons fresh
   thyme leaves
½ cup all-purpose flour
pinch of sugar
4 extra-large eggs
1¼ cups whole milk
salt
mixed salad greens, dressed
   with garlic vinaigrette,
   to serve (optional)

one

Two

Three

one Preheat the oven to 350°F. Lightly grease a 1½-quart ovenproof dish. Arrange the tomatoes in a single layer in the dish, then scatter the cheese and thyme over them and set aside.

Two Sift the flour, sugar, and a pinch of salt into a large bowl and make a well in the center. Break the eggs into the well and use a whisk or fork to blend them together. Add half of the milk and stir, gradually incorporating the flour from the side of the bowl until blended. Whisk in the remaining milk until a smooth batter forms.

Three Gently pour the batter over the tomatoes, shaking the dish slightly to distribute the cheese and thyme. Place in the preheated oven and bake for 50–55 minutes, or until the batter is puffed, golden, and set and the tomatoes are tender.

four Remove the clafoutis from the oven and let stand for 5 minutes before serving. Alternatively, let cool completely and then serve with a dressed salad, if using.

Artichauts entiers
Whole Artichokes

✤ Serves 4
✤ Prepared in 20–25 minutes,
  plus cooling
✤ Cooks in 40–45 minutes

2 lemons
4 large globe artichokes
2¼ sticks salted butter
2 tablespoons fresh thyme leaves
zest and juice of 1 lemon
salt and pepper
crusty bread, to serve

one Fill a large saucepan halfway with cold water. Halve the lemons, squeeze the juice into the water, and drop the skins in, too. Cut the stems off the artichokes near the bottom, then "scalp" them by chopping off the top 1 inch of the leaves. Add them to the water, cover, and bring to a boil. Once boiling, the artichokes will take 20–30 minutes to cook, depending on their tenderness and size. They are ready when the outer leaves can be pulled off without any effort.

Two Drain the artichokes, turn them upside down, and let cool for 15 minutes while you make the lemon-and-thyme-flavored butter. Gently melt the butter in a small saucepan, then mix in the thyme, lemon zest and juice, and salt and pepper.

three Place the artichokes in four shallow bowls and season with salt and pepper. Place the butter into four small bowls or in the removed outer leaves of the artichoke. Put a large bowl in the middle of the table for discarded artichoke pieces and leaves. Serve the artichokes and butter with crusty bread.

Tajine aux légumes

Vegetable Stew

✤ Serves 4
✤ Prepared in
  20–25 minutes,
  plus soaking
✤ Cooks in 40 minutes

2 tablespoons olive oil
1 large onion, finely chopped
3 garlic cloves, crushed
1 tablespoon ground coriander
2 teaspoons ground cumin
2 teaspoons ground ginger
¼ teaspoon crushed red pepper
large pinch of saffron threads
2 red bell peppers, seeded
  and chopped
2 cups chopped butternut
  squash flesh
1 (14½-ounce) can diced
  tomatoes
2 tablespoons tomato paste
1 cup dried apricots, figs, or
  prunes
½ preserved lemon, sliced
1 bay leaf
1 small bunch cilantro, leaves
  and stems separated, stems
  tied together and lightly
  crushed, leaves chopped and
  reserved to garnish
1¼ cups couscous
pat of salted butter
1 (15-ounce) can chickpeas,
  drained and rinsed
1 zucchini, halved lengthwise
  and sliced

large handful of baby spinach
  leaves
salt and pepper

toasted slivered almonds,
  to garnish
flatbread, to serve (optional)

one Heat the oil in a large casserole dish over medium–high heat. Add the onion and sauté, stirring, for 2 minutes. Add the garlic and sauté for an additional 1–3 minutes, or until the onion is soft. Stir in the coriander, cumin, ginger, crushed red pepper, and saffron and stir for a further 30 seconds.

Two Add the red peppers, squash, tomatoes, tomato paste, apricots, preserved lemon, bay leaf, cilantro stems, and enough water to cover all the ingredients by 3 inches. Season with salt and pepper. Cover the casserole dish and bring to the boil, then stir well, replace the cover, reduce the heat to low, and simmer for 20 minutes.

Three Meanwhile, put the couscous in a heatproof bowl. Add the butter and season with salt. Pour over enough boiling water to cover by 1 inch, place a folded dish towel over the top, and set aside until the couscous is tender and the liquid has been absorbed. Fluff with a fork and set side.

four Add the chickpeas and zucchini to the casserole dish and continue simmering for 5–10 minutes, or until the zucchini is tender. Stir in the spinach leaves and let wilt. Taste and adjust the seasoning, if necessary. Discard the bay leaf and cilantro stems. Garnish with slivered almonds and the reserved chopped cilantro leaves. Divide the couscous among four bowls and ladle the stew over the top. Serve immediately with flatbread, if using.

one

Two

Three

Aubergines au four
Baked Stuffed Eggplants

+ **Serves 4**
+ **Prepared in 40 minutes**
+ **Cooks in 40–60 minutes**

2 eggplants (about 1 pound each),
   halved lengthwise

3 tablespoons extra virgin olive oil,
   plus extra for greasing

2 onions, finely chopped

4 large garlic cloves, crushed

1 (14½-ounce) can diced tomatoes

½ cup water

3 tablespoons tomato paste

¼ cup chopped fresh flat-leaf parsley

½ tablespoon dried oregano or marjoram

pinch of sugar

½ cup cold cooked long-grain rice

¾ cup shredded Gruyère cheese
   or Swiss cheese

1 slice day-old French bread,
   ground into coarse bread crumbs

1–1½ cups tomato puree

bouquet garni of 2 parsley sprigs, 1 bay leaf,
   and 2 thyme sprigs, tied with string

salt and pepper

mixed herbs, to garnish

one Use a knife and small spoon to scoop out the eggplant flesh, leaving a ¼-inch shell all around, and set the flesh aside. Sprinkle the eggplant shells with salt and set aside for 30 minutes. Heat 2 tablespoons of the oil in a large skillet with a tight-fitting lid over medium–high heat. Add the onions and sauté, stirring, for 3 minutes. Add the garlic and continue sautéing for an additional 2 minutes, or until the onions are soft. Stir in the tomatoes, the remaining oil, the water, tomato paste, parsley, oregano, sugar, and reserved eggplant flesh and season with salt and pepper. Bring to a boil, stirring, then reduce the heat, cover, and simmer for 15–20 minutes, stirring occasionally, or until the mixture thickens. Stir in the rice.

Two Meanwhile, preheat the oven to 350°F. Grease an ovenproof dish large enough to hold the eggplant halves. Rinse the eggplant shells and pat dry. Arrange them in the prepared dish and spoon in the eggplant-and-rice mixture. Combine the cheese and bread crumbs and sprinkle over the tops. Pour just enough tomato puree into the ovenproof dish to come halfway up the sides of the eggplant shells. Tuck in the bouquet garni and season with salt and pepper. Put the dish in the preheated oven and bake for 15–20 minutes, or until the eggplant shells are tender and the cheese is melted and bubbling. Discard the bouquet garni and serve immediately, garnished with mixed herbs.

Salads & Sides

Salade au chèvre
Goat Cheese Salad

❖ Serves 4
❖ Prepared in
   10–15 minutes
❖ Cooks in 5–8 minutes

12 baguette slices
6 ounces goat cheese log,
   cut into 12 slices
4 cups mixed salad greens,
   large leaves torn into
   bite-size pieces
2 tablespoons snipped
   fresh chives
⅓ cup vinaigrette or garlic
   vinaigrette
pepper

one

two

three

one Preheat the broiler to high. Place the bread slices on a broiler rack and toast the bread slices until crisp and golden, but not dark brown. Immediately remove the broiler rack from under the broiler and turn the slices of toast over.

Two Place a slice of goat cheese on each bread slice, then return them to the broiler for 2 minutes, or until the cheese is bubbling.

three Meanwhile, place the salad greens in a large bowl with the chives, add the dressing of choice, and use your hands to toss until the leaves are coated.

four Divide the salad among individual plates, top each with three cheese-topped toasts, and serve while still hot, seasoned with pepper.

154   Salads & Sides

Salade niçoise
Tuna, Egg & Olive Salad

* Serves 4–6
* Prepared in 20–25 minutes
* Cooks in 10–15 minutes

2 tuna steaks, about ¾ inch thick
olive oil, for brushing
2½ cups green beans, trimmed

garlic vinaigrette
2 hearts of lettuce, leaves separated
3 extra-large, hard-boiled eggs, quartered
2 juicy vine-ripened tomatoes,
  cut into wedges
1 (2-ounce) can anchovy fillets in oil, drained
½ cup Niçoise olives (or ripe black olives)
salt and pepper

one Heat a ridged grill pan over high heat until you can feel the heat rising from the surface. Brush the tuna steaks with oil on one side, place the oiled side down on the hot pan, and grill for 2 minutes.

two Lightly brush the top side of the tuna steaks with a little more oil. Use a pair of tongs to turn over the tuna steaks, then season with salt and pepper. Continue grilling for an additional 2 minutes for rare or up to 4 minutes for well done. Let cool.

three Meanwhile, bring a saucepan of salted water to a boil. Add the beans to the pan and return to a boil, then boil for 3 minutes, or until tender but crisp. Drain the beans and immediately transfer to a large bowl. Pour the garlic vinaigrette over the beans and stir together, then let the beans cool in the dressing.

four To serve, line a platter with lettuce leaves. Lift the beans out of the bowl, letting the excess dressing remain behind, and pile them in the center of the platter. Break the tuna into large flakes and arrange it over the beans.

five Arrange the hard-boiled eggs and tomatoes around the side. Place the anchovy fillets over the salad, then scatter with the olives. Drizzle the remaining dressing in the bowl over everything and serve.

Salade au fenouil

Fennel Salad

✤ **Serves 4**
✤ **Prepared in 10 minutes**
✤ **No cooking**

2 oranges
1 bulb Florence fennel (or
   fennel), thinly sliced
1 red onion, sliced into
   thin rings
pepper
fennel leaves, to garnish

Dressing
juice of 1 orange
2 tablespoons balsamic vinegar

one

two

one Peel and slice the oranges, being careful to remove all of
the white pith.

two Arrange the orange slices in the bottom of a shallow dish.
Place a layer of fennel on top and then add a layer of onion.

three Mix together the orange juice and vinegar and drizzle it over
the salad. Season with pepper, garnish with fennel leaves, and serve.

three

Salade aux poivrons
Bell Pepper Salad

* ❖ Serves 4
* ❖ Prepared in 10–15 minutes
* ❖ Cooks in 8–10 minutes

2 red bell peppers
2 green bell peppers
2 yellow or orange bell peppers

½ cup garlic vinaigrette
6 scallions, finely chopped
1 tablespoon capers in brine, rinsed
6 ounces soft goat cheese,
  any rind removed
chopped fresh flat-leaf parsley, to garnish

one Preheat the broiler to high. Arrange the bell peppers on a broiler pan, position about 4 inches from the heat, and broil for 8–10 minutes, turning them frequently, or until the skins are charred all over. Transfer the bell peppers to a bowl, cover with a damp dish towel, and let stand until cool enough to handle.

Two Using a small knife, peel each of the bell peppers. Working over a bowl to catch the juices from inside the peppers, cut each bell pepper in half, remove the cores and seeds, then cut the flesh into thin strips.

three Arrange the pepper strips on a serving platter and spoon the reserved juices over them, then add the vinaigrette. Sprinkle with the scallions and capers, then crumble the cheese over the salad. Garnish with the parsley and serve.

Rosbif et crudités

Beef Salad with Crudités

❖ Serves 4
❖ Prepared in 20 minutes
❖ No cooking

2 carrots, thinly shredded
¼ cup vinaigrette
1 large cooked beet,
   thinly shredded
8 cold roast beef slices
salt and pepper
baguette and Dijon mustard
   (optional), to serve

Celeriac rémoulade
2 egg yolks
1 teaspoon Dijon mustard
1½ cups extra virgin olive oil
1 tablespoon capers in brine,
   rinsed and coarsely chopped
2 tablespoons finely chopped
   fresh flat-leaf parsley
1 tablespoon lemon juice,
   or to taste
½ head celeriac, shredded
salt and pepper

one

one

Two

one To make the rémoulade dressing, blend the egg yolks and mustard in a food processor. With the motor running, slowly add the oil, starting with just a few drips at a time, until the mixture emulsifies and forms a mayonnaise. You might not need all the oil. Transfer the mixture to a bowl and stir in the capers and parsley. Slowly add the lemon juice to taste. Season with salt and pepper. Stir the celeriac into the rémoulade and adjust the seasoning again, if necessary.

Two Put the carrots in a bowl, toss with 2 tablespoons of the vinaigrette and season with salt and pepper. Put the beet in a separate bowl, toss with 2 tablespoons of the vinaigrette and season with salt and pepper.

Three Divide the beef among four plates. Arrange a little of each of the salads alongside. Serve with baguette and a small dish of mustard, if using, on the side.

Choux braisé aux lardons

Braised Cabbage with Bacon

✤ **Serves 4**
✤ **Prepared in 5–10 minutes**
✤ **Cooks in 20–25 minutes**

2 tablespoons salted butter,
  plus extra to serve (optional)
1 tablespoon olive oil or
  sunflower oil
2 ounces smoked bacon, chopped
1 shallot, finely chopped
1 small green cabbage, tough
  outer leaves removed, cored,
  and thinly shredded
2 tablespoons caraway seeds

½ cup water or vegetable stock
salt and pepper
chopped fresh flat-leaf parsley,
  to garnish

one Melt the butter with the oil in a large skillet with a tight-fitting lid over medium heat. Add the chopped bacon and stir for 3 minutes. Add the shallot and continue sautéing for an additional 3 minutes.

two Add the cabbage and caraway seeds and stir for 3–5 minutes, or until the cabbage begins to wilt. Add the water and bring to a boil, then reduce the heat to low. Season with salt and pepper, but remember that the bacon will be salty. Cover and simmer for 10–12 minutes, or until tender.

three Uncover the skillet, increase the heat, and stir until any liquid evaporates. Adjust the seasoning and transfer to a serving dish. Garnish with parsley and add a pat of butter, if desired. Serve immediately, straight from the dish.

Endives au jambon

Belgian Endive with Ham

❖ Serves 4
❖ Prepared in 5 minutes
❖ Cooks in 12–15 minutes

2 tablespoons salted butter
2 large heads of Belgian endive,
   halved lengthwise
1 cup chicken stock or
   vegetable stock
⅓ cup chopped, cooked ham
   (trimmed of fat)
2 tablespoons heavy cream
salt and pepper
chopped fresh flat-leaf parsley,
   to garnish

one

one

two

one Preheat the oven to 225°F. Melt the butter in a large, heavy skillet with a tight-fitting lid over medium-high heat. Add the endives, cut side down, and sauté for 5 minutes, or until golden brown. Pour in enough stock to come halfway up the sides of the endives, add the ham, and season with salt and pepper (but remember that the ham might be salty). Cover the skillet and bring to a boil. Reduce the heat to low and simmer for 5–8 minutes, or until the endives are tender.

Two Use a slotted spoon to transfer the endives to an ovenproof dish and keep warm in the oven. Add the cream to the cooking liquid, bring to a boil, and boil until reduced by half. Taste and adjust the seasoning, if necessary. Spoon the sauce over the endives, garnish with parsley, and serve immediately.

Tomates farcies à l'avocat
Stuffed Tomatoes

✤ **Serves 4**
✤ **Prepared in 10 minutes**
✤ **No cooking**

12 small ripe tomatoes (about
  1¾ inches wide)
1 large ripe avocado
1 tablespoon lemon juice
¼ cup mayonnaise
6 canned anchovy fillets in oil,
  drained and finely chopped
8 pitted, ripe black olives, finely chopped
pepper
snipped fresh chives, to garnish

one Cut a thin slice from the bottom of each tomato and scoop out and discard the seeds. Place cut side down on several layers of paper towels and let drain.

Two Meanwhile, halve the avocado and remove the pit. Scoop the flesh into a bowl and mash with the lemon juice. Add the mayonnaise, anchovies, and olives. Mix well and season with pepper.

three Spoon the avocado mixture neatly into the tomatoes. Arrange on a serving plate and sprinkle with snipped chives to garnish.

Carottes à la vichyssoise

Vichy Carrots

❖ Serves 4–6
❖ Prepared in
   10–15 minutes
❖ Cooks in 10–15 minutes

2 tablespoons unsalted butter
6 carrots (about 1 pound), cut
   into ¼-inch slices
1 tablespoon sugar
bottle of Vichy mineral water
salt and pepper
2 tablespoons chopped fresh
   flat-leaf parsley

one

two

three

one Melt the butter in a large, heavy saucepan over medium–high heat. Stir in the carrots, then stir in the sugar and season with salt and pepper.

two Pour over enough Vichy water to cover the carrots by 2 inches and bring to a boil. Reduce the heat to medium and let the carrots simmer, uncovered, stirring occasionally, until they are tender, all the liquid has been absorbed, and they are coated in a thin glaze.

three Adjust the seasoning, if necessary, transfer to a serving dish, and stir in the parsley. Serve immediately.

Frites

French Fries

* ❖ Serves 4
* ❖ Prepared in 15–20 minutes, plus soaking
* ❖ Cooks in 40–45 minutes

3 large russet potatoes
  (about 1½ pounds)
sunflower oil or peanut oil,
  for deep-frying
salt and pepper

one Peel and cut the potatoes into even ½-inch sticks. As soon as they are prepared, put them into a large bowl of cold water to prevent discoloration, then let them soak for 30 minutes to remove the excess starch.

Two Drain the potatoes and dry well on a clean dish towel. Heat the oil in a deep-fat fryer or large, heavy saucepan to 375°F. If you do not have a thermometer, test the temperature by dropping a potato stick into the oil. If it sinks, the oil isn't hot enough; if it floats and the oil bubbles around the potato, it is ready. Carefully add a small batch of potatoes to the oil (this is to be sure of even cooking and to avoid reducing the temperature of the oil) and deep-fry for 5–6 minutes, or until soft but not browned. Remove from the oil and drain well on paper towels. Let cool for at least 5 minutes. Continue to deep-fry the remaining potatoes in the same way, letting the oil return to the correct temperature each time.

three When ready to serve, reheat the oil to 400°F. Add the potatoes, in small batches, and deep-fry for 2–3 minutes, or until golden brown. Remove from the oil and drain on paper towels. Serve immediately, seasoned with salt and pepper.

Gratin Dauphinois
Creamy Potato Gratin

✤ **Serves 4**
✤ **Prepared in 15 minutes**
✤ **Cooks in 1½ hours**

salted butter, for greasing
6 red-skinned or white round potatoes
   (about 1½ pounds), peeled and sliced
2 garlic cloves, crushed
1 red onion, sliced
¾ cup shredded Gruyère cheese
   or Swiss cheese
1¼ cups heavy cream
salt and pepper

one Preheat the oven to 350°F. Lightly grease a shallow 1-quart ovenproof dish.

Two Arrange a single layer of potato slices evenly in the bottom of the prepared dish. Top the potato slices with half of the garlic, half of the sliced red onion, and one-third of the shredded Gruyère cheese. Season with salt and pepper.

three Repeat the layers in exactly the same order, finishing with a layer of potatoes topped with shredded cheese.

four Pour the cream over the top of the potatoes and bake in the preheated oven for 1½ hours, or until the potatoes are cooked through and the top is browned and crispy. Serve immediately, straight from the dish.

Pommes de terre sautées

Sautéed Potatoes

❖ Serves 4
❖ Prepared in 10 minutes
❖ Cooks in 25 minutes

4 red-skinned or white round
    potatoes (about 1 pound)
¼ cup goose fat or duck fat,
    or 3 tablespoons salted butter
    with 1 tablespoon olive oil
salt

one

three

three

one Bring a large saucepan of lightly salted water to a boil. Add the potatoes, bring back to a boil, and cook for 5 minutes. Drain the potatoes and, when they are cool enough to handle, peel and cut into thin slices or small cubes.

Two Melt the fat or butter in a large, heavy sauté pan or skillet over high heat, until hot but not smoking. Pour off any excess fat so you are left with ¼ inch.

three Add the potatoes to the pan, spread out so they are evenly distributed, and reduce the heat to medium. Sauté the potatoes, shaking the pan and turning them occasionally, for 10–12 minutes, or until they are golden brown and crisp on the outside. Use a slotted spoon to transfer the potatoes to a plate lined with paper towels and drain well. Season with salt and serve immediately.

Haricots verts
Green Beans

* ❖ Serves 4
* ❖ Prepared in 5 minutes
* ❖ Cooks in 5–8 minutes

3 cups trimmed green beans
1 tablespoon sunflower oil
½ cup slivered almonds
2 tablespoons salted butter
2 teaspoons lemon juice

2 tablespoons finely chopped
  fresh flat-leaf parsley
salt and pepper

one Bring a saucepan of lightly salted water to a boil. Add the beans, bring back to a boil, and boil for 3–5 minutes, or until tender. Drain well.

two Meanwhile, heat the oil in a large skillet over high heat. Add the almonds and sauté, stirring, until golden brown, being careful that they do not burn. Set aside. Use a slotted spoon to transfer the beans to a plate lined with paper towels and drain well. Wipe out the skillet.

three Melt the butter in the skillet. Add the beans and stir. Add the lemon juice, season with salt and pepper, then stir in the parsley. Transfer the beans to a serving dish and sprinkle with the almonds to serve.

Petits pois et laitue

Peas with Lettuce

✤ **Serves 4–6**
✤ **Prepared in
   5–10 minutes**
✤ **Cooks in 15–20 minutes**

2 tablespoons salted butter,
   plus an extra pat
1 teaspoon sunflower oil
1 ounce unsmoked bacon,
   chopped
1 shallot, finely chopped
2 cups shelled peas
1¼ cups vegetable stock
   or water
1 Boston lettuce or butter
   lettuce, cored and shredded
2 tablespoons chopped
   fresh chervil
salt and pepper

one

Two

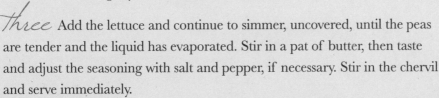

three

one Melt the butter with the oil in a large saucepan over medium heat. Add the bacon and stir for 3 minutes. Add the shallot and continue sautéing for another 3 minutes.

Two Add the peas and stock and season with salt and pepper (but remember that the bacon will be salty). Cover the pan and bring to a boil over high heat, then uncover, reduce the heat slightly, and simmer for 5 minutes.

Three Add the lettuce and continue to simmer, uncovered, until the peas are tender and the liquid has evaporated. Stir in a pat of butter, then taste and adjust the seasoning with salt and pepper, if necessary. Stir in the chervil and serve immediately.

BOULANGERIE

JOLIBERT DAMIEN

PATISSERIE

Desserts & Baking

Flan au caramel
Crème Caramel

✤ Serves 4
✤ Prepared in
  10–15 minutes,
  plus chilling
✤ Cooks in 1½ hours

unsalted butter, for greasing
1 cup superfine sugar
  or granulated sugar
¼ cup water
½ lemon
2 cups whole milk
1 vanilla bean
2 extra-large eggs
2 extra-large egg yolks

one

three

four

one Preheat the oven to 325°F. Lightly grease the bottoms and sides of four ramekins (individual ceramic dishes). To make the caramel, place a third of a cup of the sugar with the water in a saucepan over medium–high heat and cook, stirring, until the sugar dissolves. Boil until the syrup turns a deep golden brown. Remove from the heat immediately and squeeze in a few drops of lemon juice. Divide evenly between the ramekin dishes and swirl around. Set aside.

two Pour the milk into a saucepan. Slit the vanilla bean lengthwise and add it to the milk. Bring to a boil, remove the saucepan from the heat, and stir in the remaining sugar, stirring until it dissolves. Reserve.

three Beat together the eggs and egg yolks in a bowl. Pour the milk mixture over them, whisking. Remove the vanilla bean. Strain the egg mixture into a bowl, then transfer and divide evenly between the ramekin dishes.

four Place the dishes in a roasting pan. Bring a saucepan of water to a boil. Carefully pour enough boiling water into the roasting pan so that it comes two-thirds of the way up the sides of the dishes.

five Bake in the preheated oven for 1–1¼ hours, or until a knife inserted in the center comes out clean. Let cool completely. Cover with plastic wrap and chill for 24 hours.

six Run a spatula around the edge of each dish. Place an up-turned serving plate, with a rim, on top of each dish, then invert the plate and dish, giving a sharp shake halfway over. Lift off the ramekin dishes and serve.

183

Crème brûlée

- ❖ Serves 6
- ❖ Prepared in 20–25 minutes
- ❖ Cooks in 1 hour

2 cups heavy cream
1 vanilla bean
½ cup superfine sugar or granulated sugar, plus extra for the topping
6 egg yolks

one Preheat the oven to 325°F.

Two Pour the cream into a small saucepan. Split the vanilla bean in half lengthwise. Scrape the seeds into the pan, then chop the bean into little pieces and add it, too. Heat the cream to boiling, then reduce the heat and simmer gently for 5 minutes.

three Put the sugar and egg yolks in a heatproof bowl and beat with a spoon until well mixed. Pour the hot cream into the egg mixture, beating (not whisking) as you pour, until it has thickened. Pass this custard through a fine strainer into another bowl. Pour the mixture into a wide, flat dish and place it in a roasting pan. Boil a saucepan of water and carefully pour the hot water into the roasting pan so that it comes halfway up the sides of the crème brûlée dish.

four Carefully place in the preheated oven and bake for about 30–45 minutes, or until the custard has just set.

five Remove from the oven and let cool to room temperature. Sprinkle a little sugar over the custard, then gently caramelize it using a kitchen blow torch or by putting it under a hot broiler. Let cool for a few minutes, then serve.

Compôte de fruits frais

Fresh Fruit Salad

* ✤ Serves 4
* ✤ Prepared in 15 minutes, plus chilling
* ✤ Cooks in 20 minutes

1 lemon
⅓ cup superfine sugar or granulated sugar
¼ cup elderflower syrup or cordial
1¼ cups water
4 Golden Delicious, Empire, or Pink Lady apples, peeled, cored, and sliced
1½ cups blackberries
2 fresh figs, sliced

Honey yogurt
⅔ cup Greek-style plain yogurt
2 tablespoons honey

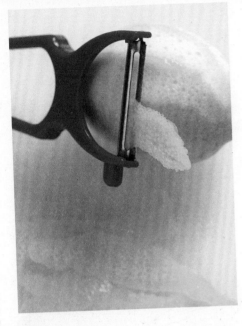

one

two

three

one Thinly pare the rind from the lemon using a vegetable peeler. Squeeze the juice. Put the lemon rind and juice into a saucepan, together with the sugar, elderflower syrup, and water. Set over low heat and simmer, uncovered, for 10 minutes.

Two Add the apples to the saucepan. Simmer gently for about 4–5 minutes, or until just tender. Remove the pan from the heat and set aside to cool.

Three When cold, transfer the apples and syrup to a serving bowl and add the blackberries. Add the figs. Stir gently to mix. Cover and chill in the refrigerator until ready to serve.

four Spoon the yogurt into a small serving bowl and drizzle the honey over the top. Cover and chill before serving. Serve the fruit salad in four small bowls, with small dishes of the yogurt alongside.

Tarte Tatin

Apple Tart

* Serves 6
* Prepared in 25–30 minutes, plus resting
* Cooks in 45–50 minutes

1 cup superfine sugar or granulated sugar
1¼ sticks unsalted butter
4 Pippin or Golden Delicious apples, peeled, cored, and sliced
1 sheet ready-to-bake puff pastry
all-purpose flour, for dusting
vanilla ice cream, to serve (optional)

one Place an 8-inch ovenproof skillet over low heat and add the sugar. Melt the sugar until it starts to caramelize, but do not let it burn, then add the butter and stir it in to make a light toffee sauce. Remove from the heat.

Two Place the apple slices in the skillet on top of the toffee sauce. The apples should fill the skillet. Put the skillet over medium heat and cover. Simmer, without stirring, for about 5–10 minutes, until the apples soak up some of the sauce, then remove from the heat.

Three Preheat the oven to 375°F. Roll out the pastry on a lightly floured surface, making sure it is large enough to thickly cover the skillet with extra space on the sides. Lay it on top of the apples and tuck the edges down between the fruit and skillet until it is sealed. Don't worry about making it look too neat—it will be inverted before eating.

four Put the skillet into the preheated oven and bake for 25–35 minutes, checking to make sure the pastry doesn't burn. The pastry should be puffed and golden. Remove from the oven and let rest for 30–60 minutes.

five When you're ready to eat, make sure the tart is still a little warm (reheat it on the stove, if necessary) and place a plate on top. Carefully invert it and lift the skillet off. Serve with some vanilla ice cream, if using.

Sablés au beurre
Rich Butter Cookies

✤ **Makes 22–24**
✤ **Prepares in 10 minutes,
plus chilling**
✤ **Cooks in 12–15 minutes**

2 cups all-purpose flour,
   plus extra for dusting
¾ cup confectioners' sugar,
   sifted
pinch of salt
1¾ sticks unsalted butter, diced
   and frozen for 10 minutes
2 extra-large egg yolks,
   beaten with ½ teaspoon
   vanilla extract
1 egg yolk, beaten with
   1 teaspoon whole milk,
   to glaze

one If you have time, put the food processor blade in the refrigerator to chill before you make the dough. Blend the flour, sugar, and salt in a food processor. Add the butter and process until fine crumbs form. With the motor running, add the vanilla egg yolks through the feed tube and process until a soft dough forms. Be careful to avoid overworking the dough. Scrape the dough out of the food processor bowl onto a lightly floured work surface and divide into two portions. Quickly knead each portion into a ball, wrap in plastic wrap, and chill in the refrigerator for at least 30 minutes.

Two Meanwhile, line two baking sheets that will fit in your refrigerator with parchment paper. Lightly flour a work surface and a rolling pin. Take one dough ball out of the refrigerator and roll out until it is ¼ inch thick. Use a floured 2½-inch round cutter to cut out 11 or 12 circles, quickly rerolling the trimmings. Brush any excess flour off the top of the dough circles and use a metal spatula to transfer them to one of the prepared baking sheets. Handle the dough as little as possible and, if it becomes soft and buttery at any point, return it to the refrigerator to chill. Place the baking sheet in the refrigerator while you roll out the remaining dough and cut out more circles. Chill all the dough circles for at least 30 minutes before baking.

Three Meanwhile, preheat the oven to 350°F. Lightly brush the cookies with the egg glaze and return them to the refrigerator while the oven heats. Bake in the preheated oven for 12–15 minutes, or until they are golden brown at the edges. Remove the baking sheets from the oven and let the cookies stand for 5 minutes, then transfer to wire racks to cool completely.

Two

Three

Three

Tarte au citron
Lemon Tart

* ✤ Serves 6–8
* ✤ Prepared in 25 minutes, plus chilling
* ✤ Cooks in 35 minutes

grated rind of 2–3 large lemons
²⁄₃ cup lemon juice
½ cup superfine sugar or granulated sugar
½ cup heavy cream or crème fraîche
3 extra-large eggs
3 extra-large egg yolks
confectioners' sugar, for dusting
fresh raspberries, to serve

Pie dough

1⅓ cups plus 1 tablespoon all-purpose flour, plus extra for dusting
½ teaspoon salt
1 stick unsalted butter, chilled and diced
1 egg yolk, beaten with 2 tablespoons ice-cold water

one To make the dough, sift the flour and salt into a large bowl. Add the butter and rub it in with your fingertips until the mixture resembles fine bread crumbs. Add the egg yolk and water and stir to mix to a dough. Gather the dough into a ball, wrap in plastic wrap, and let chill for at least 1 hour.

two Preheat the oven to 400°F. Roll the dough out on a lightly floured surface and use to line a 9–10-inch loose-bottom tart pan. Prick the bottom of the dough all over with a fork and line with parchment paper and pie weights or dried beans.

three Bake in the preheated oven for 15 minutes, or until the pastry looks set. Remove the paper and weights. Reduce the oven temperature to 375°F.

four Beat together the lemon rind, lemon juice, and superfine sugar until blended. Slowly beat in the cream, then beat in the eggs and yolks, one by one.

five Place the pastry shell on a baking sheet and pour in the filling. Transfer to the preheated oven and bake for 20 minutes, or until the filling is set.

six Let cool completely on a wire rack. Dust with confectioners' sugar and serve with raspberries.

Macarons à la vanille
Vanilla Macarons

❖ **Makes 16**
❖ **Prepared in 30 minutes, plus resting**
❖ **Cooks in 10–15 minutes**

¾ cup almond meal
   (ground almonds)
1 cup confectioners' sugar
2 extra-large egg whites
¼ cup superfine sugar
½ teaspoon vanilla extract

Filling
4 tablespoons unsalted butter,
   softened
½ teaspoon vanilla extract
1 cup confectioners' sugar,
   sifted

three

four

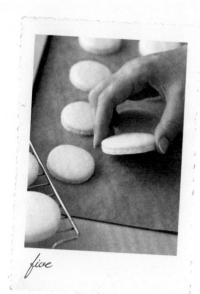

five

one Place the almond meal and confectioners' sugar in a food processor and process for 15 seconds. Sift the mixture into a bowl. Line two baking sheets with parchment paper.

Two Place the egg whites in a large bowl and beat until holding soft peaks. Gradually beat in the superfine sugar to make a firm, glossy meringue. Beat in the vanilla extract.

Three Using a spatula, fold the almond mixture into the meringue, one-third at a time. When all the dry ingredients are thoroughly incorporated, continue to cut and fold the mixture until it forms a shiny batter with a thick, ribbonlike consistency.

four Pour the mixture into a pastry bag fitted with a ½-inch plain tip. Pipe 32 small circles onto the prepared baking sheets. Tap the baking sheets onto a work surface to remove air bubbles. Let stand at room temperature for 30 minutes. Meanwhile, preheat the oven to 325°F.

five Bake in the preheated oven for 10–15 minutes. Let cool for 10 minutes, carefully peel the macarons off the parchment paper, then let cool completely.

six To make the filling, beat the butter and vanilla extract in a bowl until pale and fluffy. Gradually beat in the confectioners' sugar until smooth and creamy. Use to sandwich pairs of macarons together.

Macarons à la framboise
Raspberry Macarons

❖ **Makes 16**
❖ **Prepared in 30 minutes, plus resting**
❖ **Cooks in 10–15 minutes**

¾ **cup almond meal (ground almonds)**
1 cup confectioners' sugar
2 extra-large egg whites
¼ **cup superfine sugar**
pink food coloring

Filling
⅔ **cup heavy cream**
1 teaspoon vanilla extract
3 tablespoons raspberry preserves

one Place the almond meal and confectioners' sugar in a food processor and process for 15 seconds. Sift the mixture into a bowl. Line two baking sheets with parchment paper. Place the egg whites in a large bowl and beat until holding soft peaks. Gradually beat in the superfine sugar to make a firm, glossy meringue. Beat in food coloring until bright pink.

Two Using a spatula, fold the almond mixture into the meringue, one-third at a time. When all the dry ingredients are thoroughly incorporated, continue to cut and fold the mixture until it forms a shiny batter with a thick, ribbonlike consistency.

three Pour the mixture into a pastry bag fitted with a ½-inch plain tip. Pipe 32 small mounds onto the prepared baking sheets. Tap the baking sheets firmly onto a work surface to remove air bubbles. Use the tip of a toothpick to swirl a little food coloring through the top of each macaron. Let stand at room temperature for 30 minutes. Preheat the oven to 325°F. Bake in the preheated oven for 10–15 minutes. Cool for 10 minutes, then carefully peel the macarons off the parchment paper. Let cool completely.

four To make the filling, whip together the cream and vanilla extract until holding soft peaks. Sandwich pairs of macarons together with the vanilla cream and preserves.

197

Meringues

Meringues

✤ **Makes 13**
✤ **Prepared in 15 minutes,**
   plus cooling
✤ **Cooks in 1½ hours**

4 egg whites
pinch of salt
⅔ cup granulated sugar
⅔ cup superfine sugar
1¼ cups heavy cream, lightly
   whipped, to serve
raspberries, to serve

two

four

five

one Preheat the oven to 250°F. Line three baking sheets with sheets of parchment paper.

two Place the egg whites and a pinch of salt in a large clean bowl and, using an electric handheld mixer or a balloon whisk, beat until stiff. (You should be able to turn the bowl upside down without any movement from the beatened egg whites.)

three Beat in the granulated sugar, a little at a time; the meringue should begin to look glossy at this stage.

four Sprinkle in the superfine sugar, a little at a time, and continue beating until all the sugar has been incorporated and the meringue is thick, white, and forms peaks.

five Transfer the meringue mixture to a pastry bag fitted with a ¾-inch star tip. Carefully pipe about 26 small whirls of the mixture onto the prepared baking sheets.

six Bake in the preheated oven for 1½ hours, or until the meringues are pale golden, and can be easily lifted off the paper. Let them cool overnight in the turned-off oven.

seven Just before serving, sandwich the meringues together in pairs with the cream and arrange on a serving plate, with raspberries sprinkled around them.

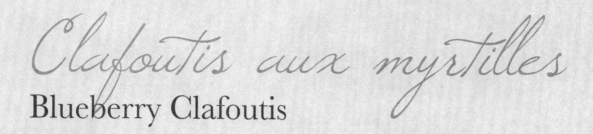

Clafoutis aux myrtilles
Blueberry Clafoutis

* Serves 4
* Prepared in 15–20 minutes
* Cooks in 30 minutes

2 tablespoons unsalted butter, softened,
  plus extra for greasing
⅔ cup superfine sugar or granulated sugar
3 eggs
½ cup all-purpose flour
1 cup light cream
½ teaspoon ground cinnamon
3 cups blueberries
confectioners' sugar, for dusting
light cream, to serve (optional)

one Preheat the oven to 350°F. Grease a 1-quart ovenproof dish.

two Put the butter in a bowl with the superfine sugar and beat together until pale and creamy. Add the eggs and beat together well. Sift in the flour, then gradually stir in the cream, followed by the cinnamon. Continue to stir until smooth.

three Arrange the blueberries in the bottom of the prepared ovenproof dish, then pour the batter over the berries. Transfer to the preheated oven and bake for about 30 minutes, or until puffed and golden.

four Remove from the oven, dust lightly with confectioners' sugar, and serve with cream, if using.

Parfait à la framboise

Raspberry Parfait

❖ **Serves 6**
❖ **Prepared in 15 minutes,**
   plus freezing
❖ **Cooks in 10 minutes**

3½ cups raspberries,
   plus extra to decorate
⅔ cup confectioners' sugar
1 tablespoon kirsch or cherry
   brandy (optional)
⅓ cup granulated sugar
½ cup water
2 egg whites
1¼ cups heavy cream

one Put the raspberries in a food processor or blender and process to form a smooth puree. Push through a nylon strainer into a bowl to remove the seeds.

Two Sift the confectioners' sugar into the raspberry puree, then stir together until well mixed. Stir in the kirsch or cherry brandy, if using.

three Put the granulated sugar and water in a small, heavy saucepan over low heat and heat gently, stirring, until the sugar has dissolved. Bring to a boil, then boil, without stirring, for 5 minutes, or until a syrup has formed. Do not let it brown. Meanwhile, beat the egg whites in a large bowl until stiff and dry.

four Drizzle the hot sugar syrup in a thin stream onto the beaten egg whites, beating all the time until the mixture is thick, creamy, and fluffy. Continue beating until the mixture is cold.

five Whip the cream until stiff. Fold the raspberry puree into the egg white mixture, then fold in the whipped cream.

six Freeze the raspberry mixture in a freezerproof container, uncovered, for 1–2 hours, or until mushy. Turn the mixture into a bowl and stir vigorously to break down any ice crystals. Return to the container and freeze for an additional 1–2 hours, or until firm. Cover the container with a lid for storing. Serve in sundae dishes, sprinkled with raspberries.

Two

three

five

203

Sorbet au Champagne

Champagne Sorbet

- ✤ Serves 4
- ✤ Prepared in 10 minutes, plus freezing
- ✤ Cooks in 5 minutes

juice of 1 lemon
1 cup water
¾ cup granulated sugar
1 tablespoon liquid glucose
1 cup Champagne
mint leaves, to decorate

one Combine all the ingredients except the Champagne in a small saucepan. Place the saucepan over low heat and stir gently until all the sugar has dissolved. Increase the heat and bring to a boil, then remove from the heat. Let cool at room temperature.

Two When cool, add the Champagne and stir in. If using an ice cream maker, pour into the ice cream maker and churn for 30–45 minutes, or according to the manufacturers' instructions.

three Alternatively, freeze the mixture in a freezerproof container, uncovered, for 1–2 hours, or until mushy. Turn the mixture into a bowl and stir vigorously to break down any ice crystals. Return the sorbet to the container and freeze for an additional 2–3 hours, or until firm. Cover the container with a lid for storing.

four When ready to serve, let the sorbet soften slightly at room temperature before serving in sundae dishes, decorated with a few mint leaves.

Mousse au chocolat

Chocolate Mousse

✤ Serves 4–6
✤ Prepared in
   10 minutes,
   plus chilling
✤ Cooks in 6–10 minutes

10 ounces semisweet dark
   chocolate, broken into small
   pieces, plus extra finely
   chopped pieces, to serve
1½ tablespoons unsalted butter
1 tablespoon brandy
4 eggs, separated

one

two

one Place the chocolate in a heatproof bowl set over a saucepan of gently simmering water. Add the butter and melt with the chocolate, stirring, until smooth. Remove from the heat, stir in the brandy, and let cool slightly. Add the egg yolks and beat until smooth.

Two In a separate bowl, beat the egg whites until stiff peaks form, then fold into the chocolate mixture. Spoon into small serving bowls or custard cups and level the surfaces. Transfer to the refrigerator and chill for at least 4 hours, or until set.

three Take the mousse out of the refrigerator and serve, sprinkled with finely chopped chocolate pieces.

two

Soufflé au chocolat
Chocolate Soufflé

❖ Serves 4
❖ Prepared in 15 minutes
❖ Cooks in 45–55 minutes

1¼ cups milk
2 tablespoons unsalted butter,
   plus extra for greasing
4 extra-large eggs, separated
1 tablespoon cornstarch
¼ cup superfine sugar or
   granulated sugar, plus extra
   for sprinkling

4 ounces semisweet dark chocolate,
   broken into pieces
½ teaspoon vanilla extract
½ cup semisweet chocolate chips
confectioners' sugar, for dusting

Chocolate custard
2 tablespoons cornstarch
1 tablespoon granulated sugar
2 cups whole milk
2 ounces semisweet dark chocolate,
   broken into pieces

one Preheat the oven to 350°F. Grease a 1-quart soufflé dish and sprinkle with the superfine sugar.

two Heat the milk with the butter in a saucepan until almost boiling. Mix the egg yolks, cornstarch, and superfine sugar in a bowl and pour in a small amount of the hot milk mixture, whisking as you pour. Transfer this cornstarch mixture to the pan of hot milk and cook gently, stirring continuously, until thickened. Add the chocolate and stir until melted. Remove from the heat and stir in the vanilla extract.

three Beat the egg whites in a clean bowl until standing in soft peaks. Fold half of the egg whites into the chocolate mixture. Fold in the rest, then stir in the chocolate chips. Pour into the prepared dish and bake in the preheated oven for 40–45 minutes, or until risen.

four Meanwhile, make the custard. Put the cornstarch and granulated sugar in a small bowl and mix to a smooth paste with a little of the milk. Heat the remaining milk until almost boiling. Pour a little of the hot milk over the cornstarch mixture, mix well, then pour the cornstarch mixture into the pan of hot milk. Cook gently, stirring, until thickened. Add the chocolate to the custard, stirring until melted. Dust the soufflé with confectioners' sugar and serve immediately with the chocolate custard.

Crêpes au chocolat
Double Chocolate Crepes

✤ Serves 4
✤ Prepared in 15 minutes,
   plus resting
✤ Cooks in 30–40 minutes

1¼ cups all-purpose flour
pinch of salt
1 cup whole milk
½ cup water
1 extra-large egg
2 tablespoons salted butter,
   melted
2 tablespoons unsweetened
   cocoa powder
3 tablespoons light cream
salted butter, for greasing

Filling
5 ounces white chocolate,
   broken into small pieces
⅔ cup light cream
1 teaspoon vanilla extract
1 ounce semisweet dark
   chocolate, coarsely grated

six

six

seven

one Sift the flour and salt into a bowl. Add the milk, water, egg, and butter and whisk to a smooth, bubbly batter.

Two Pour ½ cup batter into a liquid measuring cup and whisk in the cocoa powder and cream. Pour the remaining batter into a separate liquid measuring cup. Let both batters stand for 15 minutes.

Three Grease an 8-inch skillet and heat over medium heat. Pouring from the two separate measuring cups, swirl together the two colors of batter to just cover the skillet, covering in a fairly thin, even layer.

four Cook until the underside is golden, then flip or turn with a spatula and cook the other side until golden brown.

five Repeat this process using the remaining batter. Interleave the cooked crepes with paper towels and keep warm.

six For the filling, place the white chocolate, cream, and vanilla extract in a small saucepan over low heat and stir, without boiling, until the chocolate is melted.

seven Transfer the filling to a liquid measuring cup and pour a little of the white chocolate cream onto each crepe. Fold over, top with a sprinkle of grated dark chocolate, and serve immediately, with the remaining filling on the side.

Profiteroles

Profiteroles

* ♣ Serves 4
* ♣ Prepared in 25–35 minutes
* ♣ Cooks in 40–45 minutes

Choux pastry dough
5 tablespoons unsalted butter,
   plus extra for greasing
1 cup water
¾ cup all-purpose flour
3 eggs, beaten

Cream filling
1¼ cups heavy cream
3 tablespoons superfine sugar
1 teaspoon vanilla extract

Chocolate sauce
4 ounces semisweet dark chocolate,
   broken into small pieces
2½ tablespoons unsalted butter
⅓ cup water
2 tablespoons brandy (optional)

one Preheat the oven to 400°F. Grease a large baking sheet.

Two To make the pastry dough, place the butter and water in a saucepan and bring to a boil. Meanwhile, sift the flour into a bowl. Turn off the heat and beat the flour into the butter mixture until smooth. Let cool for 5 minutes. Beat in enough of the eggs to give the mixture a soft, dropping consistency.

three Transfer the mixture to a pastry bag fitted with a ½-inch plain tip. Pipe small balls onto the prepared baking sheet. Bake in the preheated oven for 25 minutes. Remove from the oven. Pierce each ball with a toothpick to let the steam escape.

four To make the filling, whip together the cream, sugar, and vanilla extract in a small bowl. Cut the pastry balls across the middle, then pipe the filling into the balls.

five To make the sauce, gently melt together the chocolate, butter, and water in a small saucepan, stirring continuously, until smooth. Stir in the brandy, if using.

six Pile the profiteroles into individual serving dishes, pour the sauce over them, and serve immediately.

Brioche

Brioche

✤ Makes 1 loaf
✤ Prepared in 20 minutes, plus rising and overnight chilling
✤ Cooks in 35–40 minutes

2½ cups white bread flour, plus extra for dusting
2¼ teaspoons active dry yeast
1 tablespoon superfine sugar
½ teaspoon salt
2 eggs, beaten
3 tablespoons whole milk mixed with 1 tablespoon water, heated to 110°F
6 tablespoons unsalted butter, softened, plus extra for greasing
1 egg yolk beaten with 1½ teaspoons milk, to glaze

one

two

three

one Begin this recipe the day before you want to serve the brioche. Mix together 2 cups of the flour, the yeast, sugar, and salt in a large bowl and make a well in the center. Add the eggs and the milk mixture and mix, then gradually stir in the remaining flour until a sticky, flaky dough forms. Add the butter and knead it into the dough. Continue kneading until all the butter is incorporated.

two Lightly dust a work surface with flour. Turn out the dough and knead for 5–10 minutes, or until all the flour is incorporated and the dough is smooth. Lightly grease a bowl with butter. Shape the dough into a ball and roll it around in the bowl. Cover with plastic wrap and set aside in a warm place until the dough doubles in volume, which can take up to several hours. Punch down the dough to knock out the air and roll it into a ball again. Cover the bowl with plastic wrap and chill for at least 4 hours, and up to 20 hours. Generously grease a 1-quart brioche mold and set aside.

three Place the dough onto a lightly floured work surface and lightly knead it. Cut off a piece of dough about the size of a large egg and set aside. Roll the remaining dough into a smooth ball and place it in the mold, pressing down lightly. Use floured fingers to make a wide hole in the center of the dough to the mold's bottom. Shape the remaining dough into a rounded teardrop and drop it, pointed end down, into the hole.

four Lightly glaze the dough by brushing with the egg-yolk mixture, being careful not to let it drip between the dough and the mold. Cover with a clean dish towel and let rise until the dough is puffy and risen.

five Meanwhile, preheat the oven to 400°F. Lightly glaze the brioche again. Use scissors dipped in water to make eight snips from the edge of the mold to the edge of the teardrop. Place the mold in the preheated oven and bake for 35–40 minutes, or until well risen, golden brown, and the brioche sounds hollow when tapped on the bottom. Transfer to a wire rack to cool. Serve warm or at room temperature.

Baguette

French Bread

* Makes 2 loaves
* Prepared in 30–40 minutes, plus rising and resting
* Cooks in 15–20 minutes

3⅓ cups white bread flour, plus extra for dusting
1½ teaspoons salt
2¼ teaspoons active dry yeast
1⅓ cups lukewarm water
vegetable oil, for brushing

one Sift together the flour and salt into a bowl and stir in the yeast. Make a well in the center and pour in the lukewarm water. Stir well with a wooden spoon until the dough begins to come together, then knead with your hands until it leaves the side of the bowl. Place the dough onto a lightly floured surface and knead well for about 10 minutes, or until smooth and elastic. Brush a bowl with oil. Shape the dough into a ball, put it in the bowl, and put the bowl into a plastic bag or cover with a damp dish towel. Let rise in a warm place for 1 hour, or until the dough has doubled in volume.

Two Place the dough onto a lightly floured surface, punch down with your fist to knock out air, and knead for 1–2 minutes. Cut the dough in half and shape each piece into a ball. Roll out each ball to a rectangle measuring 3 x 8 inches. From one long side of a dough rectangle, fold one-third of the dough down, then fold over the remaining third of the dough. Press gently. Fold the second dough rectangle in the same way. Put both loaves in plastic bags or cover with damp dish towels and let rest for 10 minutes. Repeat the rolling and folding twice again, letting the dough rest for 10 minutes each time.

three Lightly flour and pleat two dish towels. Gently roll and stretch each piece of dough until it is 12 inches long and an even thickness. Support each loaf on the pleated dish towels, cover with damp dish towels and let rise for 30–40 minutes. Preheat the oven to 450°F. Brush a large baking sheet with oil. Carefully roll the loaves onto the baking sheets and slash the tops several times with a sharp knife. Bake in the preheated oven for 15–20 minutes, or until golden brown. Transfer to a wire rack to cool before serving.

Croissants au beurre

Butter Croissants

❖ **Makes 12**
❖ **Prepared in
30–40 minutes, plus
rising and chilling**
❖ **Cooks in 15–20 minutes**

3⅔ cups white bread flour,
  plus extra for dusting
¼ cup superfine sugar
  or granulated sugar
1 teaspoon salt
2¼ teaspoons active dry yeast
1¼ cups lukewarm whole milk,
  plus extra if needed
2½ sticks unsalted butter,
  softened, plus extra
  for greasing
1 egg, lightly beaten with
  1 tablespoon whole milk,
  for glazing

one Preheat the oven to 400°F. Stir the dry ingredients into a large bowl, make a well in the center, and add the milk. Mix to a soft dough, adding more milk if too dry. Knead on a lightly floured work surface for 5–10 minutes, or until smooth and elastic. Let rise in a large greased bowl, covered in plastic wrap, in a warm place until doubled in size. Meanwhile, flatten the butter with a rolling pin between two sheets of wax paper to form a rectangle about ¼ inch thick, then chill in the refrigerator.

Two Knead the dough for 1 minute. Remove the butter from the refrigerator and let soften slightly. Roll out the dough on a well-floured work surface to 18 x 6 inches. Place the butter in the center, fold up the sides, and squeeze the edges together gently. With the short end of the dough toward you, fold the top third down toward the center, then fold the bottom third up. Rotate 90 degrees clockwise so that the fold is to your left and the top flap toward your right. Roll out to a rectangle and fold again. If the butter feels soft, wrap the dough in plastic wrap and chill. Repeat the rolling process twice again. Cut the dough in half. Roll out one-half into a triangle ¼ inch thick (keep the other half refrigerated). Use a cardboard triangular template with a base of 7 inches and sides of 8 inches to cut out the croissants. Repeat with the refrigerated dough.

three Brush the triangles lightly with the egg glaze. Roll into croissant shapes, starting at the bottom and tucking the point under so it does not unroll while cooking. Brush again with the glaze. Place on an ungreased baking sheet and let rest until doubled in size. Bake in the preheated oven for 15–20 minutes, or until golden brown.

one

one

three

Fougasse
Black Olive & Herb Bread

❖ **Makes 2 loaves**
❖ **Prepared in 20–25 minutes,
    plus rising**
❖ **Cooks in 25–30 minutes**

2½ **cups white bread flour,
    plus extra for kneading**
¼ **cup fine semolina,
    plus extra for dusting**

2¼ **teaspoons active dry yeast**
1½ **teaspoons sugar**
2 **teaspoons salt**
1 **cup water, heated to 110°F**
olive oil, for greasing and brushing
1 **cup pitted ripe black olives,
    finely chopped**
4½ **teaspoons herbes de Provence (optional)**
tapenade or olive oil, to serve (optional)

one Mix together the white bread flour, semolina, yeast, sugar, and salt in a bowl and
make a well in the center. Gradually stir the water into the well, drawing in flour from the
side until a soft, sticky dough forms. You might not need all the water, depending on the
flours. Place the dough onto a lightly floured work surface and knead for 5–10 minutes, or
until it becomes smooth. Shape the dough into a ball, place it in an oiled bowl, and roll it
around so it is coated in oil. Cover the bowl with plastic wrap and set aside in a warm place
until the dough has doubled in volume.

Two Preheat the oven to 450°F. Dust two baking sheets with semolina and set aside.
Place the dough onto a lightly floured work surface. Add the olives and herbs, if using, and
quickly knead until they are evenly distributed. Divide the dough into two equal portions.

three Using a greased rolling pin, roll one piece of dough into an oval, 9–10 inches
long. Dust a sharp knife with semolina and make a long vertical slit in the center of
the dough, without cutting through the edges, then make three slits on each side in a
herringbone pattern. Transfer the dough to a prepared baking sheet. Shape the remaining
dough and place on the other baking sheet. Use greased fingers to pull the slits apart, if
necessary. Lightly brush the breads with oil, being careful to brush inside the slits. Place in
the preheated oven, reduce the temperature to 400°F and bake for 25–30 minutes, or until
the loaves are golden brown and sound hollow when tapped on the bottom. Transfer to a
wire rack to cool. Serve warm, with tapenade or olive oil.